The Great Physician's Rx for Arthritis

Jordan Rubin

with Joseph Brasco, M.D.

Thomas Nelson
Since 1798

NASHVILLE DALLAS MÉXICO CITY RIO DE JANEIRO BEIJING

Published in Nashville, Tennessee. Thomas Nelson is a trademark of Thomas Nelson, Inc.

Thomas Nelson Inc. titles may be purchased in bulk for educational, business, fundraising, or sales promotional use. For information, please e-mail SpecialMarkets@ThomasNelson.com.

Library of Congress Cataloging-in-Publication Data

Rubin, Jordan.
The Great Physician's Rx for arthritis / by Jordan Rubin with Joseph Brasco.
p. cm.
Includes bibliographical references.
ISBN-10: 0-7852-1917-X (hardcover)
ISBN-13: 978-0-7852-1917-X (hardcover)
1. Arthritis—Popular works. 2. Arthritis—Religious aspects—Christianity. 3. Arthritis—Rehabilitation—Popular works. I. Brasco, Joseph. II. Title.
RC660.4.R84 2006
616.4'6206—dc22 2005036830

Printed in the United States of America

07 08 09 10 QW 6 5 4 3 2 1

Contents

INTRODUCTION

Changing Things Up

When it came to eating, Pat McCleave liked his routine.

This fifty-year-old father of two from Wichita, Kansas, kissed his wife, Tammy, and children, Tanner and Molly, good-bye each weekday morning and drove ten minutes to the McDonald's restaurant on Tyler Road for breakfast.

He was as automatic as a stoplight: five days a week, he ordered two bacon, egg, and cheese biscuits, a side of hash browns, and a thirty-two-ounce Coke—the high-octane version. After finishing his morning meal, he always replenished his plastic cup with another quart of regular Coke since refills were free.

Pat worked in a cubicle for an industrial pump company, sipping Coke while he went about his tasks as an applications engineer. By 9:00 a.m., he said, his stomach was the caramel-colored reservoir of a half gallon of Coke, meaning his intestinal tract had been given the challenge of metabolizing 620 calories and 86 grams of sugary soda pop as well as 1,026 calories from his biscuits and hash browns.

His McDonald's breakfast usually held Pat over until lunch-time, when he and several guys in the office would alternate between two mouth-watering eateries: the Hog Wild Pit Bar-B-Q, which served generous mounds of molasses-flavored smoked barbecued pork, or Chico's, an unpretentious mom-and-pop Mexican restaurant. At Chico's, Pat always ordered the #7 combination plate: beef taco, pork burrito, and cheese enchilada sitting in a shallow pool of refried beans and Spanish rice.

When his energy ran low in the middle of the afternoons, which happened often, Pat snacked on a Snickers bar while drawing on his fourth or fifth Coke that day. "I never felt like I had much energy when I got home in the evening," Pat said. "After Tammy cooked dinner, I would sit around and be unproductive, usually watching TV."

The only strength he could summon was to hold a bag of Fritos in his left hand and lift a handful of chips to his mouth with his right hand. He exercised his thumb by manning the remote.

That pretty much sums up Pat's couch-potato lifestyle for many years. He had been living with a variety of aches and pains in his joints ever since the time he helped his brother pour a concrete slab in his backyard fifteen years earlier. After getting on his hands and knees to smooth freshly poured concrete that weekend, Pat woke up the following morning with jolting pain in his left knee, so painful he could barely walk. Even standing up was painful.

"When I went to see a doctor, his first question was, 'Do you have a history of gout in the family?'" Pat recalled. "I thought for a moment. I remember my father having knee problems, but those were unrelated to gout. An uncle related to me by marriage had gout, but I always thought gout hit people in their toes, not their knees."

His doctor ran a blood test, which determined that Pat's uric acid levels were very high, a strong indicator of the disease. "You've got gout," the family physician declared.

"What do I do about it?" Pat asked.

"You should avoid organ meats and highly rich foods like lobster in butter and other shellfish. And I need to put you on some medications."

"How long do I have to take these pills?" he asked.

"You'll have to take Allopurinol every day for the rest of your life," his doctor replied. "As for Colchicine, we'll see."

The idea of taking strong meds for the next forty years didn't sit well with Pat, but what were his choices? He gulped down Allopurinol and Colchicine faithfully for the next fifteen years despite some nasty side effects: flulike symptoms, headaches, and regular bouts of diarrhea, the "bad type," he said.

Pat didn't feel that taking drugs was an acceptable way to treat his condition, but he didn't think there was a better way to wellness. All he knew was that he was putting on weight like a sumo wrestler. He slowly but steadily gained weight until he pushed the family weight scale to its limit of 360 pounds. Sure, he had tried various diets over the years and had lost "a thousand pounds easy," he said. The problem was that all those pounds came right back—and then some—once he began eating "normal food" again. "I lost weight on Atkins, on T-Factor, on the cabbage soup diet—but none of them were anything I could live with. In my desperation, I even took fen-phen diet pills. I lost tons of weight with those, but fen-phen was taken off the market because of health risks. Something to do with heart valve disorders."

Dieting was a drag, and besides, Pat liked dropping into McDonald's each morning to eat and chat with other regulars. He became friendly with a fellow named Dallas McCloud, who had heard me speak at Central Christian Church in Wichita. They shared an interest in collegiate sports: Dallas was a Kansas State fan while Pat followed archrival Kansas University. His new friend seemed to be into health food, which seemed funny since he went to McDonald's every weekday morning, but Dallas only ordered a cup of coffee and nothing to eat. "I think Dallas genuinely enjoyed the group of folks who came in each morning," Pat said.

It was at a McDonald's booth where Pat first heard Dallas talk about the Great Physician's prescription for health and wellness. The plan made sense, but Pat wasn't convinced that changing his diet to foods that God created, taking nutritional supplements, and adding exercise to his day would work for him. After all, he had tried more than a dozen "diets" over the years only to experience crushing defeat.

But years of experiencing poor health, taking anti-gout medications, and enduring the runs prompted Pat to ask his friend some questions. "Hey, Dallas, you've talked to me several times about Jordan Rubin's book. Maybe it *can* help me out. What does he suggest?"

His friend seized the opportunity and shared a plan that you will read about in *The Great Physician's Rx for Arthritis.* In the first fifty days, Pat completely changed his diet, began exercising for the first time in years, and lost fifty pounds. Amazing! He still stops by McDonald's every weekday morning, but these days he sips water while visiting with Dallas because he's already eaten a healthy breakfast at home. "I'll have a bowl of Ezekiel 4:9 cereal or cook a couple of omega-3 eggs with goat cheese before leaving the house," he said.

At lunchtime, instead of a #7 at Chico's, Pat eats with his work colleagues at a healthy café where he orders a fatoush salad with salmon or grilled tuna. For dinner, Tammy—who got on board the Great Physician's prescription as well—prepares delicious home-cooked meals using high-quality organic ingredients.

For exercise, Pat doesn't mind walking the flight of stairs from his second-story office to the company restroom on the first floor—something that happens a half dozen times a day from drinking a lot more water. After work, he and Tammy stroll around the neighborhood for fifteen or twenty minutes a day. On weekends, Pat started mowing the lawn again. After six months, he had lost a total of seventy pounds!

I'll talk more about Pat's amazing turnaround in the last chapter in this book, "Key #7: Live a Life of Prayer and Purpose," but his story of being suddenly struck by a debilitating arthritic condition has become all too widespread these days. Like age, arthritis has a way of creeping up on you until one morning that occasional stiffness in the knee or soreness in the hands turns into a "That hurts!" type of pain. Prolonged physical activity only prolongs the soreness.

Arthritis is a general medical term that refers to inflammation of the joints. The English word *arthritis* is a blend of the Greek words *arthron* for "joint" and *itis* for "inflammation." Frequent cracking of the joints and early morning stiffness are common symptoms of osteoarthritis, even during pain-free periods. Some will joke that they can tell a weather change is ahead when their knees act up, but that's because painful joints can be sensitive to a falling of barometric pressure, which signals rain in the forecast.

Arthritis often begins subtly with a little ache and stiffness in the knees or shoulders. Or it may herald its arrival with sharp pain and swollen, tender joints. Arthritis takes center stage, however, when you feel as stiff as a board while you pull yourself out of bed in the morning. Stiff spines, creaky necks, and balky backs can zap the life out of even the most optimistic individuals. Those with arthritic hands and wrists find it painful to type or even use a computer mouse, while some with arthritic knees shuffle around with pain as their constant companion. Arthritic hips not only restrict mobility but also impact a couple's love life since arthritic hip pain can make sexual relations painful, particularly for women. No matter how you cope or make lifestyle adjustments, arthritis is a pain to live with.

THE RISING NUMBERS OF ARTHRITIS

Arthritis is the most common chronic condition in the world, according to Harvard Medical School, and the most common cause of disability in the United States,.[1] Around 80 percent of people over the age of fifty show signs of degenerative arthritis, and a fourth of them experience pain. Almost half of all elderly people have arthritis, and the elderly population is the fastest-growing segment of the US population.[2] The case can be made that arthritis is the nation's primary crippler of older people.

Modern medicine doesn't fully understand why arthritis becomes more common as you grow older, but it's probably due to several factors: with age the muscles become weaker, the body adds weight, and the body's muscles and tissues are less able to heal themselves.

Arthritis rears its painful head in various ways; medical researchers have identified more than one hundred different arthritic diseases. Nearly one in six, or forty-three million Americans, suffer from the pain and joint stiffness associated with arthritis, and the Centers for Disease Control estimates that number will grow to almost one in five by 2020.[3] In terms of gender, before age forty-five more men than women have osteoarthritis, whereas after age forty-five it is more common in women, according to the National Institute of Arthritis and Musculoskeletal and Skin Diseases.

Arthritis is one of the most prevalent chronic health problems and the leading cause of disability among Americans over the age of fifteen. Seven million Americans experience limits on everyday activities like walking, dressing, and bathing due to arthritis, but contrary to conventional wisdom, arthritis is not simply a disease of the elderly. More than half of those with arthritis are under age sixty-five, and nearly three hundred thousand American children have a form of juvenile arthritis.[4]

Of the more than one hundred types of arthritis that affect areas in and around the joint, I will focus my attention on these three:

- Osteoarthritis, or OA, is the most common type of arthritis, affecting twenty million people in the United States.[5] This degenerative disease is associated with a breakdown of cartilage in the body's joints, especially those that bear the body's weight—spine, hips, knees, and toes. Cartilage, a smooth, gel-like tissue that covers the ends of bones in a joint, allows bones to glide over or rub against each other. Cartilage also absorbs energy from the shock of physical movement. When osteoarthritis develops in the joints of the body, a layer of cartilage breaks down and wears away. Suddenly, bone is rubbing against bone, causing pain, swelling, and loss of motion.

The risk of developing osteoarthritis increases dramatically as the odometer of life turns over the age of fifty. Although doctors have yet to find a cure for osteoarthritis, various treatments can relieve pain and help OA sufferers remain active.

- Gout is a form of arthritis that causes sudden, severe attacks of pain, swelling, and tenderness. Gout usually affects one joint at a time, as Pat McCleave's left knee would attest. Those afflicted with gout endure jolts of abrupt pain, and the swollen joint is warm to the touch and marked by red or purple skin.

  When doctors suspect gout, they order a blood test to check for high levels of uric acid, which are symptomatic of the disease. Uric acid in the body comes from eating various foods and easily passes through the kidneys, where it's usually processed and passed out of the body as waste. Some foods are higher in uric acid, including red meat and organ meats such as liver and kidneys, an explanation for why gout has been long attributed to be a disease of the rich and famous. While gorging on fatty food and fine wine can contribute to gout, they are not the main causes of this condition; it's the kidney's inability—partly determined by heredity—to properly flush uric acid from the body that is the culprit.

When the kidney can't keep up with uric acid in the bloodstream, uric acid crystals may form into gritty nodules and accumulate under the skin near the joint. These crystals, called tophi, are the cause of sudden spikes of pain, as Pat McCleave learned.

- Pseudogout differs from gout in that an abnormal formation of calcium pyrophosphate (CPP) crystals releases fluids into the body's joints, causing spasms of pain and severe tenderness around the joint. Pseudogout commonly affects people as they age, usually over the age of sixty. Those battling a thyroid condition, kidney failure, or calcium or iron metabolism disorders have an increased risk for gout.

There's a fourth major type of arthritis that I will not address in this book, and it's rheumatoid arthritis, a long-lasting condition that can affect other parts of the body besides the hands, wrists, and knees. Rheumatoid arthritis, the second most common form of arthritis, happens when the immune system—which normally defends the body from attack by outside viruses and bugs—mistakenly attacks itself and causes joint tissues to swell. The resulting inflammation spreads to surrounding tissues, which, like a row of dominoes, damages cartilage and bones. For this book, however, I will focus my attention on osteoarthritis and gout.

There's no doubt that osteoarthritis affects people differently.

For some, the disease progresses quickly; in others, the symptoms are more serious. Osteoarthritis tends to impact people as they age: more than half of those sixty-five and older would display evidence of osteoarthritis in at least one joint if they submitted to an X-ray.[6] Scientists have yet to discover the underlying causes of the disease, but they suspect a combination of factors:

- being overweight
- the aging process
- joint injury
- stresses on the joints from certain jobs, especially repetitive tasks
- sports activities

Osteoarthritis hurts people in more than their aching joints: their pocketbooks take a hit from the cost of treatment, prescribed medications, and over-the-counter drugs. In addition, physical activity as well as movement is curtailed, which may mean wages lost from disability. But some people would pay anything not to experience the pain of osteoarthritis, which can come and go in a capricious moment.

"One of the most interesting clinical features of osteoarthritis is the lack of correlation between the severity of osteoarthritis—as determined by degenerative changes apparent on an X-ray—and the degree of pain," reports the *Encyclopedia of Natural Medicine*. "In some cases, the joint will appear normal, with little if any joint-space narrowing, yet the pain can be excruciating. On the other hand, there are cases in which there is tremendous deformity, yet very little pain. The exact cause of the pain in osteoarthritis is still not well defined, but there are numerous potential causes. Depression and anxiety appear to increase the experience of the pain of osteoarthritis."[7]

Warning Signs

How do you know if you have osteoarthritis?

- You feel a steady or intermittent pain in a joint.
- You feel stiffness in a joint after getting out of bed or sitting for a long time.
- You experience swelling or tenderness in one or more joints.
- You have a crunching feeling in a joint or hear the sound of bone rubbing on bone.
- The skin over the joint is reddish or purple and feels warm to the touch.
- Finally, understand that you may not experience any of these painful symptoms since only one-third of the people whose X-rays show evidence of osteoarthritis report pain or other symptoms.

I'll discuss in greater detail the role of deadly emotions such as depression and anxiety later in this book, but for now, you need to know that osteoarthritis is the reason why massive numbers of people are seeking knee and hip replacement surgery. More than six hundred thousand men and women received hip and knee replacements in 2005,[8] up from a trickle just ten or fifteen years ago. That number is expected to rise as people of my parents' generation—the seventy-eight million baby boomers born from 1946 to 1964—succumb to the aches and pains of growing older. I count it a blessing that my parents—part of the baby boom cohort—haven't experienced any severe arthritic conditions. Although my mother has shown signs of arthritis in her hands, it's being controlled by following the Great Physician's prescription.

"Boomers are the first generation that grew up exercising, and the first that expects—even demands—that they be able to exercise into their seventies," said Dr. Nicholas A. DiNubile, a respected surgeon who coined and trademarked the term *boomeritis.* "Physically, though, you can't do at fifty what you did at twenty-five. We've worn out the warranty on some body parts. That's why so many Baby Boomers are breaking down. It ought to be called Generation Ouch."[9]

CONVENTIONAL TREATMENT

Modern medicine has made startling discoveries and breathtaking advances in the treatment of disease in the last century, but when it comes to arthritis, very little progress has been made. A nineteenth-century British physician, Sir William Osler, once wrote, "When a patient with arthritis walks in the front door, I feel like leaving out the back door."[10]

I would imagine that many of today's family physicians feel

the same way. When a patient walks into a doctor's office complaining of pain in one of his joints, a physician will examine his general health, checking reflexes and muscle strength. The doctor will next inspect the joint and observe the patient's ability to walk, bend, and perform routine activities. X-rays can determine how much the cartilage in the joint has deteriorated, as well as detect bone spurs.

A diagnosis of osteoarthritis is usually not a difficult call for doctors. Deciding on a treatment program is more problematic, though, since there are various approaches to manage pain and improve function. He may suggest injecting cortisone into the inflamed joint to temporarily relieve pain, but this short-term measure is generally not recommended for more than two or three treatments a year. (Besides, cortisone shots are painful because they're done with gigantic needles.) Most of the time, physicians recommend treatment plans involving exercise, rest and joint care, pain relief medications, weight control, or even surgery.

Asking patients to begin range-of-motion exercises is an inexpensive approach that sidesteps negative side effects from medications. Low-impact activities like brisk walking, swimming, and biking strengthen muscles and are easy on the joints. Going on a diet to slim down can take weight off the spine, hips, and knees, but many lack the will or the stamina to pursue a major lifestyle change that involves exercise and weight control.

This is why many physicians feel compelled to reach for their prescription pads and write out prescriptions for a class of drugs known as COX-2 inhibitors, which reduce inflammation but come with harmful reactions ranging from mild to severe. The most popular is Celebrex, which has turned out to be a blockbuster after being introduced by Pfizer in 1998. Worldwide sales of Celebrex were more than $2 billion in 2006,[11] and it's estimated that twenty-three million Americans are taking the drug.[12]

Celebrex owns the football field after two other best-selling COX-2 drugs, Vioxx and Bextra, were voluntarily withdrawn from the market in 2005 following the release of a government study that found an increased risk of heart attacks and strokes. You've probably read in the newspapers about how Merck, the drug company that brought Vioxx to market, is facing ten thousand lawsuits from plaintiffs claiming that they developed cardiovascular disease from the drug. While this legal quagmire works its way through courtrooms around the country, the US Food and Drug Administration has ordered Pfizer to stamp "black box" warnings on Celebrex's labels—the FDA's toughest warning—for its purported link to cardiovascular disease.

Many choose to stay away from the harmful side effects of prescriptive drugs by choosing from among dozens, if not hundreds, of over-the-counter (OTC) medicines. Millions wake up each morning and reach for a bottle of Advil, Motrin, or Aleve, which are nonsteroidal anti-inflammatory drugs, or NSAIDs, which have been shown to reduce the swelling and pain in tender joints. Aspirin is another NSAID that has been taken by arthritis suffers dating back to eighteenth-century England.

The problem with these OTC products is that they can irritate the stomach, causing gastrointestinal problems such as ulcers, bleeding, and perforation of the stomach or intestine. The longer one uses NSAIDs, the more likely he or she will experience mild to serious side effects. Those taking NSAIDs are counseled to gulp their two Advils with food to avoid an upset stomach.

That's why some reach for non-NSAID pain relievers such as Tylenol, Datril Extra Strength, and Tempra, which are acetaminophens that do not irritate the stomach and are less likely to cause long-term side effects. These acetaminophens, however, do not have anti-inflammatory components, which means they do not decrease or reduce arthritis inflammation.

Finally, the other over-the-counter remedy is to apply topical pain-relieving creams, rubs, and sprays directly on the skin over the joint. Heavily advertised products such as Aspercreme, Bengay, and Zostrix have given soothing relief to millions over the years, and some swear by the ointments.

Whatever relief OTC products provide is temporary, however, which is a major reason why more and more are choosing the surgical route. I already mentioned the skyrocketing numbers of those submitting to hip and/or knee replacement surgery. In the early days of knee replacement surgery, for instance, patients were told not to expect to get more than ten years out of their new knees, but new technologies have pushed that number up to fifteen or even twenty years before the artificial knee wears out. Still, doctors rarely recommend hip or knee replacement surgery for those younger than age sixty-five, which means this option would not likely be available to younger boomers like Pat McCleave.

Other types of surgical procedures can help relieve the pain and disability of osteoarthritis. A skilled orthopedic surgeon can remove loose pieces of bone and cartilage from the joint, smooth out bones that are touching each other, and even reposition joints. After surgery and rehabilitation, the patient usually feels less pain and swelling, and can move around more easily.

ALTERNATIVE MEDICINE

Those who aren't eager to take medications with potential side effects or submit to hip or knee replacement surgery often seek out alternative approaches to dealing with their osteoarthritis pain.

Acupressure, a traditional Chinese medicine technique, involves placing physical pressure by hand or elbow on different pressure points on the surface of the body to bring about relief through greater balance and circulation of fluids. Proponents believe that acupressure can be quite helpful in reducing arthritis pain. *Prescription for Natural Cures* suggests that those practicing acupressure with OA patients should be sure to press the tender joints firmly instead of massaging them, working the appropriate points two or three times a day for up to six months. A light drainage massage of the areas surrounding the arthritic joint will reduce the buildup of lymphatic fluid.

Folk Remedies, Anyone?

The medical treatment of osteoarthritis is a fairly recent development in the history of mankind. In centuries past, if you woke up each morning with creaky joints as you pulled yourself out of your straw bed, there wasn't much you could do about your debilitating pain.

According to the *PDR Family Guide to Nutrition and Health*, people tried the following remedies centuries ago:

- covering themselves in cow manure twice a day
- standing naked under a full moon
- keeping two sesame seeds in the navel while they slept overnight
- enduring scores of bee stings
- tolerating the venom of snakes
- rubbing WD-40 on the skin

Wait a minute—they didn't have WD-40 during the Renaissance. That's right, but that hasn't stopped modern-day arthritis suffers from spraying a little silicone lubricant on where it hurts.[13]

A folk remedy that's more popular today is pouring a box of golden raisins into a plastic container and covering the raisins with gin. After letting the high-octane gin soak into the raisins for several weeks, you begin eating nine a day to relieve arthritis pain.

Octogenarian radio icon Paul Harvey is said to have started the gin-soaked raisin craze back in the mid-1990s by talking about it on his radio program. No scientific studies have proven that gin-soaked raisins ease arthritic pain, although if you eat enough of them, you might *forget* that you have arthritis!

Acupuncture, which is the insertion of fine needles into specific points on the body, has its supporters as well. Many of these points are near nerves, so that when stainless steel needles are inserted into the skin, the body releases chemicals called endorphins that block pain. These endorphins block the message of pain being delivered to the brain.

There are approximately 6,500 licensed acupuncturists in the US and three-thousand doctors who perform acupuncture as part of their medical practice, according to the WebMD Web site. Some insurance companies are covering this drug-free way to minimize pain.

For those suffering from gout, devil's claw has proven effective in reducing the inflammation of connective tissues, according to the *Encyclopedia of Natural Healing*. Devil's claw, as well as dandelion, dispels uric acid for those with gout. This herbal drug gets its odd name from a plant that is shaped like a claw and is grown in the savannas of southern Africa. Yucca, which comes from a form of cactus found in the southwestern part of the United States, is recommended for the relief of joint pain as well. Another herbal remedy is to rub juniper oil on tender joints to reduce inflammation.

Finally, some have found relief by wearing magnetic bracelets. The efficacy of magnets has not been proven by scientific scrutiny, but several theories abound. Some say that since blood contains iron, the blood acts as a conductor of magnetic energy, which increases the delivery of oxygen and nutrients to inflamed tissues. Magnets might affect how nerve cells respond to pain.

Anecdotal testimonies abound for the use of magnets. The PGA Champions Tour, which is comprised of over-fifty golfers like Tom Watson, Greg Norman, Fred Funk, and Jay Haas, is a hotbed of, well, magnetic beds. National golf magazines have published stories about players like Jim Colbert, who unrolls a portable mattress of magnets on top of every hotel bed when he retires each evening. Hershel Sarbin and Jim Brown, writing on the PGATour.com Web site, said:

> There have been studies with very specific populations (polio patients, people with degenerative knee pain, women with low back pain, diabetic patients) in which magnets have been shown to have a therapeutic effect. There have been just as many studies—some involving the same areas of the body—showing absolutely no benefits. There is no lack of golfers who say they have benefited by strapping magnets onto their bodies. The bad news is that magnets can be expensive, and there is no conclusive proof that they work. If they do, science has to catch up with public acceptance of the concept.[14]

WHERE WE GO FROM HERE

I recommend a total lifestyle program for the health of the body, mind, and spirit that's much more effective than sleeping on a bed of magnets each night, and it's based on the seven keys to unlock your God-given health potential found in my foundational book *The Great Physician's Rx for Health and Wellness:*

- Key #1: Eat to Live
- Key #2: Supplement Your Diet with Whole Food Nutritionals, Living Nutrients, and Superfoods

- Key #3: Practice Advanced Hygiene
- Key #4: Condition Your Body with Exercise and Body Therapies
- Key #5: Reduce Toxins in Your Environment
- Key #6: Avoid Deadly Emotions
- Key #7: Live a Life of Prayer and Purpose

Some of these keys may not seem to directly relate to arthritic conditions, but they are part of living a healthy lifestyle and can reduce pain and tenderness in the joints and the rest of the body. I'm one of those who believes that osteoarthritis requires a positive attitude. This is the time to focus on your abilities, not your disabilities. This is the time to break down activities into smaller tasks. And this is the time to plan and develop daily routines that maximize your quality of life and minimize your disability.

I am convinced that your osteoarthritis can be stopped dead in its tracks and even reversed, as Pat McCleave experienced. Better health won't happen overnight, but it can happen quickly by adopting the seven keys as your new lifestyle. I'm confident the Great Physician's prescription can work for you because I've spoken to or received e-mails from plenty of folks describing how the Great Physician's prescription is helping them live the life they've always dreamed of.

I believe each and every one of us has a God-given health potential that can be unlocked only with the right keys. I want to challenge you to incorporate these timeless principles and allow God to transform your health as you take on arthritis and reclaim your life.

Key #1

Eat to Live

One of the great stories in Scripture happened when Moses, perched on a nearby hill, watched Joshua lead the nation of Israel against the Amalekites in battle. The Bible records that as long as Moses held up a rod in his hands, Israel was winning the battle. When he rested his arms at his sides, the soldiers of Amalek were winning.

Here's how Exodus 17:12–13 (NLT) describes what happened next:

> Moses' arms finally became too tired to hold up the staff any longer. So Aaron and Hur found a stone for him to sit on. Then they stood on each side, holding up his hands until sunset. As a result, Joshua and his troops were able to crush the army of Amalek.

Centuries later, it's fun to speculate that God's chosen leader couldn't hold up the heavy bar because his shoulders suffered from osteoarthritis pain. Perhaps he should have asked Aaron to run down to the corner drugstore to pick up a tube of Bengay to ensure Joshua and his troops' glorious victory.

I'm teasing, of course, because the Old Testament informs us that when Moses died at the age of 120, his eyesight was perfect and he was strong as a young man (Deut. 34:7). Moses and the millions who followed him into the wilderness weren't racked by arthritic knees, crooked backs, and sore hands during the time of the Exodus. The psalmist declared that there wasn't one "feeble among His tribes" (Ps. 105:37 NKJV).

I'm reasonably confident that Moses and the Hebrews were in excellent shape from their natural and healthy diet as well as their physical labors, so they didn't have excess pounds increasing stress on their weight-bearing joints. Their lean bodies subsisted on a nutritious diet comprised of a wondrous array of natural fruits and vegetables and grass-fed beef and lamb. Scripture also tells us what the Israelites *didn't* eat, which was unclean and "detestable" meats such as pork, shellfish, and certain birds like vultures. While I'm not prepared to say that Moses and the Hebrews were arthritis-free since they ate so healthily, the following question is relevant today: Can the foods you eat *cause* arthritis?

The Arthritis Foundation states that this is one of the most common questions asked by people with arthritis. People naturally wonder if their chronic joint pain is the result of eating something they shouldn't have since the symptoms of arthritis often change from one day to the next. Those having a "bad day" question whether their arthritis pain was caused by something they chewed and swallowed hours earlier.

I believe arthritis can be affected by what you've dined on lately, but it's more likely caused by the cumulative effect of your lifelong diet. Just ask Doris Bailey. This fifty-six-year-old mother of two heard me speak at Calvary Temple Worship Center in Modesto, California, where I had been invited to share a message during the Sunday morning services about presenting our bodies as living sacrifices.

I challenged those in the congregation that morning: "Can you say, 'This is the best I have, and I'm giving it to the Lord'? Are you an example of God's best? Can others see your vitality? Wouldn't it be awesome if God's people were so full of good health, so vibrant, that others would notice us from ten or twenty feet away?"

Doris didn't want to be noticed because of her weight. At 330 pounds, she knew her health was far from vibrant. Decades of trolling country buffets and feasting on fried foods, jelly-filled doughnuts, and half gallons of ice cream in one sitting had taken their toll. Her knees were shot from osteoarthritis: the only way she could walk was with the assistance of a cane or walker.

After hearing me speak, Doris jumped on the Great Physician's bandwagon—well, *jumped* might not be the operative word since her arthritic knees weren't up to the challenge, but she wholeheartedly climbed aboard and completely changed her diet and lifestyle. She said she started feeling much better a month or two after following God's plan for healthy eating, which makes sense to me. I'm confident that anyone with osteoarthritis can benefit from eating whole, natural, and organic foods that are part of the Great Physician's prescription.

A nutritional approach to arthritis will go a long way toward controlling this disease. A University of North Carolina at Chapel Hill School of Medicine study suggested that those with osteoarthritis can reduce the inevitable pain and restricted movement by altering their diets. This North Carolina study reported that beta-cryptoxanthin, lutein, and lycopene, which are dietary carotenoids common in yellow and orange fruits and vegetables, appeared to reduce the odds of osteoarthritis of the knee by 30 to 40 percent, while diets heavy in soybean and other oils rich in omega-6 fatty acids as much as doubled the risk of knee problems.[1]

"Dietary practices have a major impact on arthritis," agree the authors of *Arthritis: An Alternative Medicine Definitive Guide.* "In fact, if you eat the typical American diet, it could be making your arthritis worse. Among the offenders are white flour and sugar, conventionally raised red meat, chemical additives, yeast, and conventional pasteurized and homogenized milk and dairy products. These foods can increase inflammation, invoke allergies, and interfere with hormone production, cellular integrity, and the function and mobility of the joints."[2]

My view of the relationship between osteoarthritis and diet prompts me to make three points:

1. Diet can be extremely important for keeping inflammation down.
2. Eliminating processed foods and replacing them with healthy whole and organic foods will improve your overall health, which will improve your arthritic condition.
3. Following the Great Physician's prescription, as Pat McCleave and Doris Bailey discovered, often results in significant weight loss, which will reduce undue strain on the joints. A great deal of evidence shows that being overweight increases the risk of developing osteoarthritis, especially in the knees.

Changing your diet, as well as drinking a *lot more* water, will work wonders for those aches and pains you may feel when you get out of bed in the morning. For those reasons, *The Great Physician's Rx for Arthritis* relies heavily on my first key, "Eat to Live." You can change the way you eat by doing two things:

1. Eat what God created for food.
2. Eat food in a form that is healthy for the body.

Following these two vital concepts will give you a great shot to beat arthritis and put you on the road toward living a healthy, vibrant life.

BACK TO THE SOURCE

Do you have to think hard to remember the last time you bit into a fresh apple, scooped up a handful of raisins, or supped on lentil soup? These foods are nutritional gold mines and contain no refined or processed carbohydrates, no additives or preservatives, and no artificial sweeteners. Since God has given us a bountiful harvest of natural foods to eat, it would take several pages to describe all the fantastic fruits and vibrant vegetables available from His garden. A diet based on whole and natural foods fits within the bull's-eye of eating foods that God created in a form healthy for the body.

I believe God gave us physiologies that crave these foods in their natural state because our bodies are genetically set for certain nutritional requirements by our Creator. Our taste buds, however, have been manipulated by major food conglomerates, restaurant chains, and fast-food eateries that sweeten meats with secret sauces and top everything in sight with melted cheese and bacon. The strategy has worked: we've become a country that loves inexpensive, deep-fried, greasy food that is high in calories, high in fat, high in sugar, and—in most people's minds—high in taste.

Pat McCleave's story is all too common these days: every weekday morning he sat down before a tray of McDonald's bacon, egg, and cheese biscuits and a side of fried hash browns. For him, taste trumped health, no matter how many calories or grams of trans-fatty acids the fast-food breakfast fare contained. This explains why drive-thru chains and sit-down restaurants are purveyors of cheese-and-egg sandwiches, monster burgers, buckets of fried chicken, and stuffed-crust pizza—foods not in a form that God created.

Having an awareness of what you eat is an important first step in dealing with arthritis. As we begin traveling down this road together, I want to help you understand that everything you eat is a protein, a fat, or a carbohydrate—nutrients that keep the body running as best it can. Each of these nutrients positively or negatively affects your weight and your health.

Let's take a closer look at these macronutrients.

THE FIRST WORD ON PROTEIN

Proteins, one of the basic components of foods, are the essential building blocks of the body. All proteins are combinations of twenty-two amino acids, which build body organs, muscles, and nerves, to name a few important duties. Among other things, proteins provide for the transport of nutrients, oxygen, and waste throughout the body and are required for the structure, function, and regulation of the body's cells, tissues, and organs.

Our bodies, however, cannot produce all twenty-two amino acids that we need to live a robust life. Scientists have discovered that eight essential amino acids are missing, meaning that they must come from other sources outside the body. It just so happens that animal protein—chicken, beef, lamb, dairy, eggs, and so on—is the only complete protein source providing the Big Eight amino acids.

Yet the conventional wisdom among traditional *and* alternative medicine is that animal protein contains large quantities of fat, which raise levels of inflammatory compounds in the body and increase arthritic symptoms. Trimming red meat from the diet is often promoted as a strong first step to getting osteoarthritis under control. Some folks in the alternative medicine world counsel patients not to eat any animal protein at all, saying that eating meat only worsens inflammation in the joints.

I'm not in favor of a vegetarian diet, however. While plant foods are extremely beneficial for us, they do not contain all the essential amino acids found in animal proteins, which play an important part in retaining muscle strength and keeping the immune system healthy. At the same time, I believe arthritis is a condition where cutting back on commercially produced meat consumption could work in your favor. The authors of *Arthritis: An Alternative Medicine Definitive Guide* point out that commercially produced, corn-fed meat is high in arachidonic acid, which is converted by the body into powerful pro-inflammatory compounds.[3] Arachidonic acid is a fatty acid found primarily in meat, poultry, and dairy products, and when your diet is tilted too heavily toward these foods, arachidonic acids are stored in cell membranes that instigate inflammation.

I'm confident that those battling arthritis have been eating the *wrong* kinds of meat for many years, as well as too much of it. For instance, hamburger is a high-fat meat found in every main dish from backyard burgers to spaghetti and meatballs. But in this country, the vast majority of hamburger is comprised of ground chuck with added fat from hormone-injected cattle eating pesticide-sprayed feed laced with antibiotics.

You would be much better eating hamburger—as well as other cuts of beef—produced from range-fed and pasture-fed cows. Natural beef is much healthier for you than assembly-line "production" cuts filling our nation's supermarket meat cases. The best and most healthy sources of meat come from organically raised cattle, sheep, goats, buffalo, and venison. Grass-fed beef is leaner and lower in calories than grain-fed beef, and the flavor is tremendous. Organic beef is higher in heart-friendly omega-3 fatty acids and important vitamins like B_{12} and E. When they are eaten in moderation, I don't believe lean red meats will exacerbate arthritic conditions.

For those seeking to reduce their consumption of red meat, an excellent replacement is fish, which provide nutrients that can benefit arthritis conditions. Salmon and other cold-water fish contain high levels of beneficial essential fatty acids such as omega-3s. When you eat a fresh filet of fish, omega-3 fatty acids are converted into prostaglandins, which are hormone-like fatty acids that bring on a multitude of biochemical reactions, including the reduction of inflammation in the joints.

You should shop for fish with scales and fins caught in the wild from oceans and rivers rather than "feedlot salmon" raised on fish farms, which don't compare to their cold-water cousins in terms of taste or nutritional value. While it's great to see more people eating the tender pink meat of farm-raised Atlantic salmon, it's never going to nutritionally match what comes from the wild. The salmon from fish farms spend several years lazily circling concrete tanks, fattening up on pellets of salmon chow, not streaking through the ocean eating small marine life as they're supposed to.

The better alternative is to purchase fresh salmon and other fish from your local fish market or health food store. Look for the label "Alaskan" or wild-caught. Wild-caught fish is an absolutely incredible food and should be consumed liberally. Supermarkets and health food stores are stocking these types of foods in greater quantities these days, and, of course, they are found in natural food stores, fish markets, and specialty stores.

THE SKINNY ON FATS

Since many people who suffer from osteoarthritis and gout are overweight, they look to a low-fat, reduced-fat, or fat-free diet as a panacea to lose weight and reduce the strain on their tender joints.

I don't blame anyone for thinking this way. For the last decade or so, the mainstream media has been filled with stories about how bad fat is for you. The underlying message of these news features is *if you want to lose weight, then eliminate foods with fat.* Best-selling books such as *The Pritikin Principle* by Nathan Pritikin and *The Ornish Diet* by Dean Ornish, M.D., have preached the gospel of low-fat, high-carbohydrate diets. About five years ago, we began seeing supermarket shelves filled with convenience foods displaying the magic words *fat-free* or *reduced fat* on the packaging.

Young girls nagged their mothers to buy these low-fat foods, believing they would be as thin as a Parisian supermodel if they dipped low-fat cookies into no-fat (or skim) milk. Funny how that didn't work.

What happened is that consuming low-fat blueberry muffins and reduced-fat ice cream didn't help anyone lose weight, and the case can be argued that the *opposite* happened because, statistically speaking, we've become *fatter* as a nation since the mid-1990s. The problem with snacking on reduced-fat potato chips and fat-free yogurt is more than their poor taste: it turns out that these convenience foods have nearly the same amount of calories as the full-fat versions. Since people thought they were consuming low-fat, healthy food, they ate with abandon, which caused many to gain weight.

Generally speaking, low-fat diets have several things working against them. First of all, most people cannot stay on a low-fat regimen for any length of time. "Those who possessed enough will power to remain fat-free for any length of time develop a variety of health problems including low energy, difficulty in concentration, depression, weight gain, and mineral deficiencies," wrote Mary Enig, Ph.D., and Sally Fallon in *Nourishing Traditions.*[4]

In my view, low-fat diets fail to distinguish between the

so-called good fats in food (including olive and flaxseed oils, tropical oils such as coconut oil, and fish oils) and bad fats (hydrogenated oils found in margarine and most packaged goods). We need certain fats in our diet to provide a concentrated source of energy and source material for cell membranes and various hormones. Fats also provide satiety; without them, we would be hungry within minutes of finishing a meal.

The so-called bad fats we don't need are mainly hydrogenated and partially hydrogenated fats found in processed foods, which fill cupboards and refrigerators in homes from Portland, Maine, to Portland, Oregon. I'm talking about frosted flakes for breakfast, a glazed doughnut at break time, fried corn chips and chocolate chip cookies for lunch, and breaded fried chicken nuggets for dinner.

These types of fats aren't good if you're dealing with arthritis. "The wrong kind of fats can increase inflammation in joints, while the 'good' fats will keep inflammation in check," say the authors of *Arthritis: An Alternative Medicine Definitive Guide.*[5]

When it comes to eating the right fats, I'm referring to foods loaded with the following:

- omega-3 polyunsaturated fats
- monounsaturated (omega-9) fatty acids
- conjugated linoleic acid (CLA)
- healthy saturated fats containing short- and medium-chain fatty acids, such as butter and coconut oil

These good fats are found in a wide range of foods, including salmon, lamb, goat meat, dairy products derived from goat's milk, sheep's milk, cow's milk from grass-fed animals, flaxseeds, walnuts, olives, macadamia nuts, and avocados.

The problem with the standard American diet is that people eat too many of the wrong foods containing the wrong fats and not enough of the right foods with the right fats. When it comes to cooking, the top two fats and oils on my list are extra virgin coconut and olive oils, which are beneficial to the body and don't tend to increase inflammation. I urge you to cook with extra virgin coconut oil, which is a near-miracle food that few people have ever heard of.

Coconut oil is packed with antioxidants and reduces the body's need for vitamin E. You can tell which oil is better by comparing how fast canola oil or safflower oil becomes rancid when sitting at room temperature. Coconut oil shows no signs of rancidity even after a year at room temperature.

When moms heat up or fry food these days, however, they usually pour safflower, corn, or soybean oil (any of which may be partially hydrogenated) into the pan. In the process of hydrogenation, hydrogen gas is injected into the oil under high pressure to make the oil solid at room temperature, which prevents the oil from becoming rancid too quickly. Adulterating the oil carries a price: the hydrogenation process produces trans-fatty acids, also known as *trans fat.* Trans fat has recently become a household word since the Food and Drug Administration, beginning in 2006, required new nutritional facts labels on all foods to state the amount of trans fat in them. Several municipalities, including New York City, have passed laws banning restaurants from servings foods cooked with trans fats.

Food conglomerates routinely utilize hydrogenated oil in their manufacturing plants, which means that trans fats are found in nearly all our processed foods—foods that God definitely did *not* create. I'm talking about frozen pizza, ice cream, potato chips, cookie dough, white bread, dinner rolls, snack foods, doughnuts, candy, salad dressing, margarine—the list is endless. Why do food producers employ so much chemistry? Because it allows them to produce a more competitively priced product with a longer shelf life. Commercially prepared fried foods, like French fries and onion rings, also contain gobs of trans fat, which is why KFC, Wendy's, Chili's, and Ruby Tuesday have gotten rid of trans fats from their menus.

While oils and foods with trans fat should be eliminated from your diet, I can assure you that fats and oils created by God—as you would expect—are fats you want to include in your diet.

Thinking of Trying a Special Diet?

When it comes to arthritis, no special diet will "cure" arthritis. Please don't think of the Great Physician's prescription for eating as a diet because it's more of a lifestyle change. This attitude is more in line with the etymology of our word *diet*, which originated from the Greek word *diaita*, meaning "life, lifestyle, way of living."

Still, you may hear about a special eating plan that's just the ticket for tender joint pain. The authors of *The Arthritis Cure* outlined three diets that have gained popularity among arthritis sufferers:[6]

1. *The No Nightshade Vegetables Diet.* Not eating any nightshade vegetables has been touted as a way to reduce joint pain. Some examples of nightshade vegetables, which grow in the cover of night rather than during daytime hours, are tomatoes, potatoes, eggplant, and peppers. These vegetables contain solanine, an alkaloid that interferes with enzymes in the muscles and is thought to have a negative effect on calcium balance, which could cause pain and discomfort in the bones and joints.

   Proponents say that eliminating these vegetables from your diet relieves arthritis pain, but there is no hard scientific evidence to support the connection between nightshade vegetables and arthritis. WebMD.com says the diet probably isn't harmful, but there are no studies to support it.

2. *The Dong Diet.* A physician, Collin Dong, M.D., recommends this eponymous diet, which is patterned after what Chinese peasants eat. The Dong Diet excludes sugar, coffee, red meat, herbs, tomatoes, alcohol, and dairy products, but there's no evidence that this diet works specifically against arthritis.

3. *The Alfalfa Diet.* A natural diet rich in alfalfa is said to reduce the symptoms of arthritis. I don't know how one successfully swallows a lot of alfalfa,

> but eating high amounts of a certain food to the exclusion of a well-rounded diet will never be as healthy as following the Great Physician's Rx for Arthritis Battle Plan.

DEALING WITH CARBS

The third and final macronutrient is carbohydrates, which, by definition, are the sugars and starches contained in plant foods. Sugars and starches, like fats, are not bad for you, but the problem is that the standard American diet includes way too many foods containing these carbohydrates. Sugar and its sweet relatives—high fructose corn syrup, sucrose, molasses, and maple syrup—are among the first ingredients listed in staples such as cereals, breads, buns, pastries, doughnuts, cookies, ketchup, and ice cream.

When carbohydrates are eaten, the digestive tract breaks down the long chains of starches into single sugars, mainly glucose, which is a source of immediate energy. If these calories are not expended through physical effort, the body converts them to fat, and therein lies a weighty problem. As a culture, we are a little taller but a lot heavier than we were a generation ago; today we weigh twenty-five pounds more than our grandparents or parents did in the 1960s, with the biggest weight gains attached to men forty and older.

I've come up with a surefire formula that illustrates how you can develop arthritis:

weight gain + age × lack of physical activity = tender joints and arthritis pain

That's why I've been saying all along that losing weight is a great place to start in your fight against arthritis. There's nothing you can do to stop the inexorable march of Father Time, but everyone can make a resolution to exercise more. (I'll have more to say about exercise and physical fitness in Key #4, "Condition Your Body with Exercise and Body Therapies.")

Returning to the first item in the equation—weight gain—millions of Americans battled their bulging waistlines by following low-carb diets like Atkins, South Beach, and the Zone. This trio of popular diets differs in the details, but generally speaking, they all call for an increase in high protein from sources such as meat, fish, and dairy and a reduction in the intake of carbohydrates like bread, pasta, and rice, which causes the body to burn excess body fat for fuel.

Low-carb eating has had quite a following in the last few years. The low-carb craze peaked in early 2004 when more than 9 percent of US adults claimed to be on a low-carb diet, according to market research firm NPD Group. That figure, however, declined to 2.2 percent a little more than a year later, the same time Atkins Nutritionals, the company distributing Atkins products, announced that it was seeking bankruptcy protection.[7]

It doesn't surprise me that the low-carb boom fizzled since the only good thing about low-carb diets was that people avoided excess sugar and white flour. Despite the fact that each of the aforementioned diets has some good recommendations, my biggest beef with low-carb diets is that most of these health plans advocate a high consumption of meat products that the Bible calls detestable, allow only limited amounts of nutrient-rich fruits and vegetables, and encourage the consumption of artificial sweeteners and preservatives. Replacing processed foods with natural and organic foods and consuming carbohydrates such as fruits, vegetables, nuts, seeds, legumes, and cultured dairy products are a much better way to lose weight and stay healthy.

I must note that Barry Sears, Ph.D., author of *The Zone,* did a good job describing the benefits of balancing proteins, fats, and carbs in his book, *The Anti-Inflammation Zone.* According to Dr. Sears, each of the aforementioned three major nutrients triggers a complex set of hormonal responses in the body. Eating the right foods at the right time keeps these hormones in a favorable balance. He adds that it usually takes a year before the Zone approach becomes engrained in your lifestyle.

I believe you get there quicker by eating the healthiest, most nutritious food possible right away. The foundation of the Great Physician's prescription key "Eat to Live," means that the following top healing foods should find a way into your pantry or refrigerator.

The Top Healing Foods

I've discussed many healthy foods in this chapter so far, but the following are musts when combating arthritis. (I address the best foods to eat when you have gout later in this chapter.)

Keep this in mind when you sit down to eat: you should consume the protein, fats, and vegetables first before swallowing any fruit, sweeteners, or high-starch carbohydrates like potatoes, rice, grains, and bread. I know it's hard to resist fresh bread when it's presented in a nice restaurant, but you would be better off having a piece toward the end of your meal—or better yet, not at all.

1. Wild-caught fish. As I mentioned, the omega-3 fatty acids in fish help decrease inflammation. Besides salmon caught in the cold-water Alaskan wilderness, the following fish are high in essential fatty acids: bluefish, capelin, dogfish, herring, mackerel, sardines, anchovies, shad, sturgeon, whitefish, and tuna. Be sure to look for tuna advertised as being low in mercury and high in omega-3 fatty acids. Canned tuna, which has long been the darling of the weight conscious, has been the subject of much disdain due to high levels of heavy metals, including mercury. There is now available a low mercury, high omega-3 tuna that is extremely healthy and safe to consume a few times per week. (See the Resource Guide at www.BiblicalHealthInstitute.com for recommended brands.)

2. Chicken soup with spices. If you're scratching your head, you can stop because chicken soup is good for the soul. (Wait a minute—that would make a great title for a series of books!) Stephen Rennard, M.D., chief of pulmonary medicine at the University of Nebraska Medical Center in Omaha, says that chicken soup acts as an anti-inflammatory because it apparently reduces the inflammation that occurs when coughs and congestion strike the respiratory tract.

Dr. Rennard conducted a full-blown study on the medicinal qualities of chicken soup for the common cold. He had his wife prepare a batch using a recipe from her Lithuanian grandmother. Then he carted the homemade chicken soup to his laboratory, where he combined some of the soup with neutrophils, or white blood cells, to see what would happen. As Dr. Rennard suspected, his wife's homemade chicken soup demonstrated that neutrophils showed less of a tendency to congregate, but at the same time, these neutrophils did not lose any of their ability to fight off germs.[8]

As for arthritis, research is pointing to the chicken cartilage used in making homemade soup as the anti-inflammatory agent, which is great news for your sore and aching joints. Chicken cartilage contains type 2 collagen, and according to Jean-Jacques Dugoua, ND, doctor of naturopathic medicine in Canada, the body creates immune complexes that attack the joint during bouts of arthritis. "Recent research, however, has provided evidence that the signal to attack joints in the body could possibly be retrained through the intake of chicken collagen type II," he wrote. "The theory behind the use of chicken cartilage revolves around retraining the immune system to no longer attack itself, thereby no longer attacking the cartilage in the joint."[9]

My wife, Nicki, who's a wonderful cook, and I have come up with an excellent recipe that we call tongue-in-cheek "Arthritis-Bustin' Chicken Soup." This recipe was inspired by my good friend Sally Fallon, author of *Nourishing Traditions*:

Arthritis-Bustin' Chicken Soup

1 whole chicken (free range, pastured, or organic chicken)
2–4 chicken feet (optional)
3–4 quarts cold filtered water
1 tablespoon raw apple cider vinegar
4 medium-sized onions, coarsely chopped
8 carrots, peeled and coarsely chopped
6 celery stalks, coarsely chopped
2–4 zucchinis, chopped
4–6 tablespoons extra virgin coconut oil
1 bunch parsley
5 garlic cloves
4 inches grated ginger
2–4 tablespoons Celtic Sea Salt
1/4–1/2 teaspoon cayenne pepper

Directions:

If you are using a whole chicken, remove fat glands and the gizzards from the cavity. By all means, use chicken feet if you can find them. Place chicken or chicken pieces in a large stainless steel pot with the water, vinegar, and all vegetables except parsley. Let stand for 10 minutes before heating. Bring to a boil and remove scum that rises to the top. Cover and cook for 12 to 24 hours. The longer you cook the stock, the more healing it will be. About 15 minutes before finishing the stock, add parsley. This will impart additional mineral ions to the broth.

Remove from heat, and take out the chicken and the chicken feet. Let it cool, and remove chicken meat from the carcass, discarding the bones and the feet. Drop the meat back into the soup.

3. Fruits and vegetables. Certain dietary carotenoids, which are compounds found in some fruits and vegetables, can reduce inflammation through antioxidant effects, according to a University of Manchester (United Kingdom) study that appeared in the *American Journal of Clinical Nutrition* in 2005.[10]

I mentioned a few of these carotenoids earlier in this chapter. According to the University of Manchester study of 25,000 participants, beta-cryptoxanthin and zeaxanthin lowered the risk of developing arthritis. Beta-cryptoxanthin is found in yellow or orange fruits and vegetables. The 5aday.org Web site states the following yellow or orange fruits are high in carotenoids:

- yellow apples
- apricots
- cantaloupes
- yellow figs
- grapefruit
- lemons
- mangoes
- oranges
- papayas
- peaches
- yellow pears
- pineapples
- tangerines

The following orange or yellow vegetables are recommended as well:

- butternut squash
- carrots
- yellow summer squash
- sweet corn

- yellow peppers
- yellow potatoes
- pumpkins
- sweet potatoes
- yellow tomatoes
- yellow winter squash

I don't think you can eat too many fruits and vegetables when you're battling arthritis. Be sure to include plenty of dark, leafy vegetables like spinach, parsley, and broccoli, which contain glutathione (GSH), a powerful antioxidant and detoxifying agent. Asparagus, one of the most nutritionally balanced vegetables God created, also contains glutathione.

In the fruit area, fresh pineapple from Hawaiian fields contains a key enzyme called bromelain, which reduces inflammation. Some professional coaches recommend that their athletes eat pineapple after sustaining an injury. You should always eat fresh pineapple, not the canned variety.

Grapes are recommended because resveratrol is present in the skin of red grapes, which helps block cell inflammation. Harris H. McIlwain, M.D., and Debra Fulghum Bruce, MS, authors of *Pain-Free Arthritis: A 7-Step Program for Feeling Better Again*, wrote:

> In the past few years, various studies have shown that resveratrol blocks cell inflammation, which is linked to arthritis and other diseases. A team of researchers now concludes that trans-resveratrol blocks the activation of the gene identified as COX-2, which is important in creating the inflammation that causes arthritis pain. Some

> believe that trans-resveratrol may turn out to be an improvement on aspirin in fighting diseases associated with COX-2, such as arthritis. For now, snack on grapes. They are low in fat and calories, and add some healing nutrients to your body.[11]

I'm also bullish on berries—raspberries, blueberries, blackberries, cranberries, and cherries—because they contain natural oxidants like fiber, folate, magnesium, potassium, and vitamin C to reduce inflammation.

Michael Murray, ND, author of *The Encyclopedia of Healing Foods,* says those with arthritis must have a diet rich in fruits and vegetables because their natural plant compounds can protect against cellular damage, including damage to the joints.

4. Ginger. This superstar spice deserves its own category. Ginger, the world's most widely cultivated spice, contains anti-inflammatory compounds called gingerols and natural chemicals that stimulate the production of anti-inflammatory agents like eicosanoids. "One of the body's most important chemical reactions involves compounds called eicosanoids," wrote Paul Schulick, author of *Ginger: Common Spice & Wonder Drug.* "When these elements derived from dietary fat are out of balance, many different diseases can evolve. Two of the most threatening are heightened inflammation . . . to a person who is susceptible to arthritis . . . the results of this imbalance could be devastating."[12]

Schulick suggests pouring a cup of boiling water over two tablespoons of freshly grated ginger and letting it steep for five to ten minutes. Then add a dash of hot sauce, or the juice of one lemon, and one to two tablespoons of raw honey, depending on your preferred taste. Sip throughout the day. Ginger can also be used to season foods.

Another common spice, turmeric, has been found to act as a COX-2 inhibitor without the harmful side effects seen in pharmaceutical drugs. This may explain why so many people experience relief from arthritis pain by taking substantial doses of turmeric.

5. Water. Water isn't a food, of course, but only God could come up with a liquid that makes up 92 percent of your blood plasma and 50 percent of everything else in the body. This calorie-free and sugar-free substance performs many vital tasks for the body: regulating the body temperature, carrying nutrients and oxygen to the cells, protecting organs and tissue, removing toxins, and—noteworthy for those suffering from arthritis—cushioning joints.

Did you know that your cartilage is approximately 80 percent water? Cartilage, which covers and separates the bone structures in a joint, needs water to lubricate the body's joints during movement. When cartilage is well hydrated, the two opposing surfaces glide freely, minimizing joint pain caused by bone rubbing on bone. Dehydrated cartilage increases friction between the joints, causing an inflammatory process that results in joint deterioration and pain.

F. Batmanghelidj, M.D., author of *You're Not Sick, You're Thirsty!*, says when a joint becomes dehydrated because the individual does not drink enough water, its gliding ability is diminished. "The cartilage cells sense their dehydration and give out alarm signals of pain, because they will soon die and peel off from their contact surfaces of the bones if used in their dehydrated state," he wrote. "This type of pain has to be treated with a regular increase in water intake until the cartilage is fully hydrated and washed of its acidity and toxins."[13]

This is the time to set a water bottle on your desk or kitchen counter and take a sip every ten minutes. You need to drink a minimum of eight glasses of water a day to keep those joints hydrated. Sure, you'll go to the bathroom more often, but is that so bad compared to having constant joint pain or even using a walker like Doris Bailey had to do?

I've taken this "drink plenty of water" advice to heart because I don't want to develop osteoarthritis when I get older. I set a forty-eight-ounce bottle of water on my office desk as a reminder to keep putting fluids into my system. My record for drinking water is one and one-quarter gallons of water in a day during a fast, but I won't reveal how many trips I made to the bathroom. Drinking water all day long is not only healthy for the body, but it's a key part of the Great Physician's Rx for Arthritis Battle Plan (see page 74), so keep a water bottle close by and drink water before and during meals.

6. Apple cider vinegar. You may have noticed that I included apple cider vinegar in the Arthritis-Bustin' Chicken Soup recipe. There was a reason for that, and it's because I believe apple cider vinegar is an important substance to drink when you have arthritis pain.

Apple cider vinegar is made from squeezed liquid of crushed

apples. Sugar and yeast are added to the liquid to start the fermentation process, which turns the sugar into alcohol. During a second round of fermentation, the alcohol is converted by acetic acid-forming bacteria into vinegar. The acetic acid gives vinegar its sour taste, as well as its minerals: potassium, phosphorus, calcium, magnesium, natural silicon, pectin, and tartaric acids, which help the body maintain its vital acid-alkaline balance. The acidity in apple cider vinegar helps the body rebalance its acid level, which is important as the body tries to find its equilibrium after fighting off cold and flu viruses. The icky taste hasn't stopped aficionados from singing the praises of apple cider vinegar, or ACV for short.

The "Johnny Appleseed" of apple cider vinegar is a Vermont physician, D. C. Jarvis, M.D., who injected the lore of folk medicine into his practice. His book, *Folk Medicine,* has sold more than three million copies over the last fifty years.

Remember, don't drink apple cider vinegar unless it is well diluted. I recommend two to three teaspoons of ACV and one to two teaspoons of honey mixed in eight to twelve ounces of water; otherwise, you'll be puckering your lips and shaking your head from the tartness of the first sip.

Final thought: some arthritis sufferers have found relief soaking an arthritic hand or foot in a warm or hot solution of water and ACV (at a 6:1 ratio).

7. Cultured dairy products from goats, cows, and sheep. Medical doctors lump the saturated fats in dairy products in the same category as red meat, implicating the fat intake as one of the key factors behind arthritis. Thus, doctors recommend that we should not eat full-fat dairy products. When reaching for a half gallon of milk at the supermarket, they say, be sure to choose a low-fat version like 2 percent or skim milk.

I don't see things the same way because 2 percent or skim milk is less nutritious, less digestible, and can cause allergies. I recommend dairy products derived from goat's milk and sheep's milk rather than cow's milk, although dairy products from organic or grass-fed cows can be excellent as well. The reason I prefer goat's milk and goat's cheese lies in the structure of goat's milk: its fat and protein molecules are tiny in size, which allows for rapid absorption in the digestive tract. Goat's milk is less allergenic because it does not contain the same complex proteins found in cow's milk.

Let me address one more product that directly relates to joint health—eggs. One of the first items those with chronic arthritis are told to strike off their grocery list is eggs because of the high cholesterol levels. That advice never made sense to me because eggs are a wonderful food deserving Hall of Fame status. This nutrient-dense food is packed with essential fatty acids that help control inflammation, thanks to the building blocks of prostaglandins, a bit of vitamin B12, vitamin E, lutein, riboflavin, folic acid, calcium, zinc, and iron that are found in a mere seventy-five calories.

I believe you can safely eat two eggs a day, but I strongly urge you to buy organic eggs high in omega-3, which have become much more available in response to consumer demand. Natural food markets stock them, of course, but you'll find organic eggs at major supermarket chains as well as warehouse clubs like Costco.

I urge you not to overlook cultured dairy products, such as yogurt and kefir, which provide an excellent source of easily digestible protein, B vitamins, calcium, and probiotics.

8. Green tea. David Buttle, Ph.D., a scientist in matrix biology at the University of Sheffield in the United Kingdom, has found that compounds in green tea called EGCG (epigallocatechin gallate) and ECG (epicatechin gallate) can block the enzyme that destroys cartilage. "If you have fairly severe joint damage it may be too late to do anything about it, but if you spend decades of your life drinking green tea in the end it may be beneficial," said Dr. Buttle. "Green tea should be drunk as a prophylactic, to prevent disease."[14]

More research needs to be done, but scientists believe that the antioxidants in green tea may prevent and reduce the severity of osteoarthritis. Drinking several cups of green tea a day can help to diminish the inflammation it causes.

Infusions of herbs and spices such as teas have been a part of nearly every culture throughout history. In fact, consuming organic teas and herbal infusions several times per day can be one of the best things you can do for your health. Teas and herbal infusions can provide energy, enhance the immune system, improve digestion, help you wind down after a long day, and provide the body with antioxidants such as polyphenols, which help reduce cellular damage and oxidative stress.

You'll find in the Great Physician's Rx for Arthritis Battle Plan (see page 74) that I recommend a cup of hot tea and honey with breakfast, dinner, and snacks. I also advise consuming freshly made iced green tea, as tea can be consumed hot or steeped and iced. Please note that while herbal tea provides many great health benefits, nothing can replace pure water for hydration. Although you can safely and healthfully consume two to four cups of tea and herbal infusions per day, you still need to drink at least six cups of pure water for all the good reasons I've described in this section.

WHAT ABOUT GOUT?

The Great Physician's prescription for eating takes a different tack when it comes to gout. Known as the only form of arthritis unquestionably linked to diet, this painful disorder is caused by buildup of uric acid in the bloodstream. Although gout has been dismissed as a "rich man's disease," that description is out of date. Years ago Daddy Warbucks might have dug into inch-high, heavily marbled steaks that he washed down with a fine Bordeaux, but these days, just about anyone can afford a New York strip and a glass of red wine. This means that guys from any economic class are susceptible to gout. Yes, I said *guys* on purpose because gout is nine times more likely to hit men than women.[15]

Since gout mainly occurs in men who are overweight and indulge regularly in rich foods and alcohol, those battling gout *must* limit their consumption of meat because an overload of animal protein can cause painful uric deposits in the joints. Uric acid is created from the breakdown of purine, a molecule found in DNA. Foods high in purine are liver, kidney, sweetbreads (the thymus gland), lobster, fish roe, mussels, scallops, anchovies, peas, dried beans, mushrooms, gravies, roasted nuts, beer, and other adult beverages. Foods made from refined white flour contain high levels of uric acid.

If you're drinking alcohol, you should go on the wagon because alcohol increases the production of uric acid. Intake of refined carbohydrates—cakes, rolls, muffins, and white bread—must come to a standstill. Anything with sugar, corn syrup, and fructose should be banished from your diet.

The dietary key to gout is upping consumption of anti-oxidant-rich fruits, vegetables, and apple cider vinegar. Fish such as salmon are beneficial because of their fatty acids, and you shouldn't be afraid to eat sardines and herrings because they are high in omega-3 essential fatty acids. Other foods like eggs, milk, flaxseed, olives, and nuts are low in purine and possess some anti-inflammatory benefits.

This is the time to take the Great Physician's prescription to heart. Those with gout *must* reach for a water bottle throughout the day because the only way to remove uric acid from the body is through the kidney, whose function is to remove wastes from the body. Without enough water to do the job, uric acid—and crystals—collects in the toes and knees, causing attention-getting gout pain. Drinking plenty of water allows the kidneys and liver to operate at full capacity and flush waste and toxins out of the body's joints, which is where uric acids tend to congregate.

What about Fasting?

If you do an advanced search on the Arthritis Foundation Web site (www.arthritis.org) with keyword *fasting* under the category of "Conditions and Treatment" for arthritis, you come up with nothing. In fact, the conventional medical community doesn't have much to say about fasting, which is a mistake. I'm a firm believer in the value of giving the body time off while your immune system shores up its defenses against arthritic invaders. Fasting also induces significant anti-inflammatory actions in the body.

When I talk about fasting, I think it's better—and more realistic—to concentrate on completing a one-day partial fast once a week, something I do regularly. If you've never voluntarily fasted for a day, I urge you to try it—preferably toward the end of the week. I've found that Thursdays or Fridays work best for me because the week is winding down and the weekend is coming up. For instance, I won't eat breakfast and lunch so that when I break my fast and eat dinner that night, my body has gone between eighteen and twenty hours without food or sustenance since I last ate dinner the night before.

An added benefit from fasting is how it helps you lose weight, which can take pressure off weight-bearing joints.

THE DIRTY DOZEN

When you have joint pain, there are certain foods that should never find a way onto your plate or into your hands. Here are what I call the Dirty Dozen:

1. "Detestable" or "unclean" meats and pork products. In all of my previous books, I've consistently pointed out that pork—America's "other white meat"—should be avoided because pigs were called "unclean" in Leviticus and Exodus. God created pigs as scavengers—animals that survive just fine on any farm slop, water swill, and animal waste tossed their way. Pigs have a simple stomach arrangement: whatever a pig eats goes down the hatch, straight into the stomach, and out the back door in four hours max. They'll even eat their own excrement, if hungry enough.

Even if you decide to keep eating commercial beef instead of the organic version, I absolutely urge you to stop eating pork. Read Leviticus 11 and Deuteronomy 14 to learn what God said about eating clean versus unclean animals, where Hebrew words used to describe "unclean meats" can be translated as "foul" and "putrid," the same terms the Bible uses to describe human waste.

2. Shellfish and fish without fins and scales, such as catfish, shark, and eel. Am I saying au revoir to lobster thermidor and sayonara to shrimp tempura? That's what I'm saying. You can bet your scampi.

Shellfish and fish without fins and scales, such as catfish, shark, and eel, are also described in Leviticus 11 and Deuteronomy 14 as "unclean meats." God called hard-shelled crustaceans such as lobster, crabs, shrimp, and clams unclean because they are "bottom feeders," content to sustain themselves on excrement from other fish. To be sure, this purifies water but does nothing for the health of their flesh—or yours, if you eat them.

3. **Hydrogenated oils.** This means margarine and shortening are taboo, as well as any commercial cakes, pastries, desserts, and anything with the words *hydrogenated* or *partially hydrogenated* on the label. Hydrogenated oils contain trans-fatty acids, which can lead to inflammation, one of the major risk factors for arthritis.

4. **Artificial sweeteners.** Aspartame (found in NutraSweet and Equal), saccharine (Sweet 'N Low), and sucralose (Splenda) are chemicals several hundred times sweeter than sugar. In my book, artificial sweeteners should be completely avoided whether they come in blue, pink, or yellow packets.

5. **White flour.** White flour isn't a problematic chemical like artificial sweeteners, but it's virtually worthless and not healthy for you.

6. **White sugar.** Since sugar suppresses your immune system, this unhealthy carbohydrate should be severely restricted.

7. **Soft drinks.** Run, don't hide, from this liquefied sugar. A twelve-ounce cola is the equivalent of eating nearly nine teaspoons of sugar. Soft drinks contain phosphoric acid, which can lead to gout and other health conditions resulting from overacidity.

8. **Pasteurized homogenized skim milk.** As I said, whole organic milk is better, and goat's milk is best. To give the immune system a real boost, I recommend cultured dairy products.

9. Corn syrup. This is another version of sugar and just as bad for you.

10. Hydrolyzed soy protein. If you're wondering what in the world this is, hydrolyzed soy protein is found in imitation meat products. Stick to the real stuff.

11. Artificial flavors and colors. These are never good for you under the best of circumstances, and certainly not when you're battling osteoarthritis or gout.

12. Excessive alcohol. Long-term, excessive drinking damages every organ in the body (especially the liver), adds weight, produces heart problems, promotes depression, causes digestive problems (ulcers, gastritis, and pancreatitis), and impacts fertility. And it's a prime cause of gout.

EAT: What Foods Are Extraordinary, Average, or Trouble?

I've prepared a comprehensive list of foods that are ranked in descending order based on their health-giving qualities. The best foods to serve and eat are what I call "Extraordinary," which God created for humans to eat and offer the best chance not to develop arthritis. If you are battling osteoarthritis or gout, however, it is best to consume foods from the Extraordinary category more than 75 percent of the time.

Foods in the Average category should make up less than 25

percent of your daily diet. If you're in the throes of arthritis pain, consume these foods sparingly.

Foods in the Trouble category should be consumed with extreme caution. If you are dealing with arthritis, you should avoid these foods completely.

For a complete listing of Extraordinary, Average, and Trouble foods, visit www.BiblicalHealthInstitute.com/EAT.

℞ THE GREAT PHYSICIAN'S RX FOR ARTHRITIS: EAT TO LIVE

- *Eat only foods God created.*
- *Eat foods in a form that is healthy for the body.*
- *Consume liberal amounts of homemade Arthritis-Bustin' Chicken Soup.*
- *Consume spices such as ginger and garlic daily.*
- *If you have a fever, it's best to consume lots of fluids and very little food.*
- *Consume foods high in omega-3 fatty acids.*
- *Consume foods high in fiber.*
- *Increase consumption of raw fruits and vegetables.*

- *Avoid foods high in sugar.*
- *Avoid foods containing hydrogenated oils.*

Take Action

To learn how to incorporate the principles of eating to live into your daily lifestyle, please turn to page 74 for the Great Physician's Rx for Arthritis Battle Plan.

Key #2

Supplement Your Diet with Whole Food Nutritionals, Living Nutrients, and Superfoods

If you ask a doctor whether taking multivitamins and nutritional supplements is important in the prevention or treatment of arthritis, he or she will probably reply that supplements lack solid scientific evidence in the fight against this chronic joint disease.

I view this cautious reaction as a form of defensive medicine that fails to recognize the enormous potential of—and growing evidence for—nutritional supplements with regard to arthritis. Besides, those battling persistent arthritis pain must know something is working: 64 percent of *Arthritis Today* readers said they had used a nutritional supplement in the last six months compared to 49 percent of the general population.[1]

From the outset, though, please know that I'm not one who believes arthritis or gout can be turned around with a bottle of pills. After years of study in naturopathic medicine and nutrition, I understand better than most that dietary supplements are just what they say they are—supplements, not a substitute for an inadequate diet, a lack of exercise, and an unhealthy lifestyle.

Still, nutritional supplements, whole food nutritionals, living nutrients, and superfoods are an important part of the Great Physician's prescription for arthritis. The nutritional supplements receiving the most attention these days are glucosamine and chondroitin sulfate, which are often sold in combination form by supplement companies and promoted as effective relief in reducing osteoarthritis pain.

Glucosamine and chondroitin are two naturally occurring substances found in the body. Glucosamine, which combines glucose, nitrogen, and hydrogen, is an amino acid that works against joint inflammation and rebuilds cartilage. Chondroitin, on the other hand, gives cartilage its elasticity. In supplement form, most of the glucosamine sold today is derived from the outer shells of shellfish such as crab, lobster, or shrimp. Chondroitin is extracted from cartilage harvested from cows, chickens, or sharks.

Jason Theodosakis, M.D., a physician and assistant professor at the University of Arizona School of Medicine in Tucson, suffered a sports injury that brought on osteoarthritis in the early 1990s. He began taking a daily dose of 1,500 mg of glucosamine and 1,200 mg of chondroitin—and eventually got back out on the tennis court. His personal brush with arthritis prompted Dr. Theo, as he likes to be called, to become a world-class authority on the clinical use of dietary supplements, especially glucosamine and chondroitin, for arthritis. He authored a book, *The Arthritis Cure.*

So should arthritis sufferers take glucosamine and chondroitin? The Arthritis Foundation notes that past studies have shown that some people with mild to moderate osteoarthritis who took either glucosamine or chondroitin sulfate reported pain relief at a level similar to that of nonsteroidal anti-inflammatory drugs (NSAIDs) such as aspirin and ibuprofen. Some research indicates that the supplements might also slow cartilage damage in people with osteoarthritis.

A long-awaited National Institutes of Health–funded research trial released in 2006 was expected to make a definitive statement on the use of glucosamine and chondroitin, but that didn't happen. "Conflicting media interpretation—some saying these dietary supplements work, and others saying they're a waste of money—leave consumers stranded between two extremes," a Knight Ridder news report said.[2]

According to the six-month-long, double-blind NIH trials, those taking glucosamine and chondroitin were no better off than those taking a placebo in reducing knee pain. But a smaller number of participants with moderate to severe knee pain said that a glucosamine-chondroitin combination worked 25 percent better than a placebo for pain relief.

My bottom line: glucosamine and chondroitin are safe and would be well worth trying except for the fact that most glucosamine is made from the shells of biblically detestable animals. However, you can now find supplements derived from a non-shellfish source of glucosamine. (For more information, visit www.BiblicalHealthInstitute.com and click on Resource Guide.) If you decide to try glucosamine and chondroitin, however, I urge you not to use supplements made from shellfish (glucosamine) or shark (chondroitin) but instead an enzymatically produced glucosamine and/or a more natural version of chondroitin produced from chicken collagen type II.

No matter what form of glucosamine you use, you should be aware that most people do not see results until they've taken glucosamine and chondroitin for at least two months.

THE BEST ROUTE TO TAKE

Also topping my list is omega-3 cod-liver oil because of its high concentrations of omega-3 fatty acids that reduce the production of prostaglandins and leukotrienes that reduce inflammation and promote joint lubrication. Dr. Barry Sears, author of *The Anti-Inflammation Zone,* said that the first published journal describing the benefits of high-dose fish oil as a treatment for arthritis appeared way back in 1775. Back in the old days, people said that cod-liver oil "lubricated the joints."

Omega-3 cod-liver oil contains four nutrients that reduce the markers of inflammation. These four nutrients are eicosapentaenoic acid (EPA), docosahexaenoic acid (DHA), vitamin A, and vitamin D. Vitamin A is extremely important to the health and integrity of the mucosal linings of the body, while vitamin D inhibits pro-inflammatory molecules, according to a University of Bonn clinical trial in 2006.[3]

Omega-3 cod-liver oil is the Rodney Dangerfield of nutrition—it doesn't get a lot of respect. A lot of people say they have to hold their noses to take a spoonful, but cod-liver oil comes in lemon mint and other flavors that mask the odor and taste, as well as high-quality capsules. Sure, omega-3 cod-liver oil may be as old as the hills and not real fancy, but study after study shows that people who use omega-3 cod-liver oil are less likely to develop arthritis.

Enzyme-based supplements such as bromelain and papain are also helpful in neutralizing prostaglandins, the hormones that spark pain in the body's nerve cells. As I mentioned in Key #1, bromelain is found naturally in pineapple (and papain is derived from papaya), but supplements contain higher concentrations of these inflammation-fighting compounds. Several studies provide preliminary evidence that these proteolytic enzymes might be helpful for various forms of chronic pain, including neck pain and osteoarthritis.[4]

Another supplement worth trying is *Boswellia serrata,* which comes from a tree that yields gum when its bark is peeled away. You may recognize the other name that *Boswellia serrata* goes by—frankincense, one of the special gifts that the Magi brought when they visited Jesus (see Matt. 2). If you try *Boswellia serrata,* you may find this herb is better than discovering an unexpected gift under the tree on Christmas morning because of the way it inhibits the production of leukotrienes, which cause inflammation.

Boswellia serrata, ginger, and turmeric are examples of herbs that have been used to treat arthritis for thousands of years by practitioners of Ayurveda, the traditional medicine of India. Modern medicine is taking notice. The American College of Rheumatology performed a randomized, double-blind trial of ninety people with osteoarthritis, and those who were given a combination of *Boswellia serrata,* ginger, and turmeric experienced significant and sustained pain relief.[5] Whether you sprinkle liberal amounts of ginger and turmeric in your foods or ingest them through supplementation, there's a strong chance you'll find relief from your inflammation.

A Well-Rounded List

I've long been an advocate of natural supplements, which are known in the industry as "whole food" or "living" versions. These vitamins and supplements contain different compounds such as organic acids, antioxidants, and key nutrients. They are more costly to produce since the ingredients—fruits, vegetables, sea vegetables, seeds, spices, vitamins, minerals, and so forth—are put through a fermentation process similar to the digestive process of the body, but they are well worth the extra money. Taking a whole food or living multivitamin is a great way to start off your day.

Another whole food supplement finding more favor is astaxanthin, which has been called "red gold from the sea" since it's produced from microalgae harvested off the Kona coast of Hawaii and is five hundred times stronger than vitamin E, another popular antioxidant. Antioxidants combat excessive free radical damage, which has been implicated in countless diseases and is a prime cause of inflammation. Astaxanthin, a carotenoid-based antioxidant, has not been the subject of many studies yet, but a small study released in 2006 showed that the supplement reduced systemic inflammation in the body.[6]

Another vitamin worth looking into is vitamin K, which is found naturally in spinach, cabbage, cauliflower, and other green vegetables. Epidemiological studies conducted at the Boston University School of Medicine have shown a correlation between high vitamin K intake and a reduction in the risk of osteoarthritic knee problems by 40 percent.[7]

While we're on the subject, I'm a fan of green foods because of the high concentration of vitamin K. Green foods are an array of barley grass, wheat grass, oat grass, and alfalfa grass, and they are often sold in health food stores as "green machine food," "superfood," or "perfect food." If you're having trouble motivating yourself to eat your veggies, I know a way your body can receive more green foods, which contain nutrients not found in the typical low-carbohydrate diet. I recommend the consumption of green superfood powders and caplets. All you do is mix the powder in water or your favorite juice or swallow a handful of caplets.

℞ THE GREAT PHYSICIAN'S RX FOR ARTHRITIS: SUPPLEMENT YOUR DIET WITH WHOLE FOOD NUTRITIONALS, LIVING NUTRIENTS, AND SUPERFOODS

- *Follow this nutritional supplement protocol:*

1. *Glucosamine derived from a non-shellfish source*
2. *Chondroitin contained naturally in chicken collagen type 2*
3. *Concentrations of the following spice extracts: Boswellia serrata, ginger, and turmeric*
4. *Proteolytic enzymes including bromelain and papain*

5. *Omega-3 cod-liver oil (consume one to three teaspoons or three to nine capsules of omega-3 cod-liver oil per day)*

6. *A whole food or living multivitamin as directed two or three times a day*

7. *Green superfood mixed in water or your favorite juice or in caplet form*

Take Action

To learn how to incorporate the principles of supplementing your diet with whole food nutritionals, living nutrients, and superfoods into your daily lifestyle, please turn to page 74 for the Great Physician's Rx for Arthritis Battle Plan.

Key #3

Practice Advanced Hygiene

I will be the first to admit that dipping your face into a basin of facial solution, cleaning under your fingernails with a special soap, or washing your hands after going to the bathroom doesn't sound like it has much to do with chronic arthritis pain.

But there's an aspect of good hygiene that's relevant to this discussion, and it's the role of the immune system in your body. Your immune system, which is sensitive as a cat's whisker to changes in the body's defense capabilities, is subject to attack when germs and foreign agents enter the body. "Protection against infection is vital," said Kenneth Seaton, Ph.D., an Australian scientist who has studied the link between hygiene and good health for decades. "Not only do microbes damage the joints, but many can induce the immune system to attack the joints."[1]

When Dr. Seaton researched the link between arthritis and advanced hygiene, he discovered that mucus and saliva have similar proteins and sugars to the connective tissues and lubricating fluids of the joints. "It may be this mucus and saliva, combined with germs under the fingernails and self-inoculated, may stimulate autoimmunity, which then damages cartilage and joints," he wrote in his book *Life, Health, and Longevity.*

The idea in practicing a system called *advanced hygiene* is that need to protect ourselves from the germs we pick up through everyday actions: shaking hands with others or touching handrails, doorknobs, shopping carts, paper money, coins, and food. Once germs establish a beachhead on your fingertips, it's a matter of time before you rub your eyes, scratch your nose, stroke your ears, or touch your mouth—a process known as self-inoculation.

Dr. Seaton said that ear, nose, and throat problems, which represent 80 percent of visits to doctors' offices, can be linked to how we touch our noses, eyes, mouths, and skin with dirty fingernails throughout the day. "Germs don't fly; they hitchhike," Dr. Seaton declared, and when germs hitch a ride on your fingertips, your body's immune system falls under attack as the germs, like soldiers assaulting the beaches of Normandy, invade the portals to your body. Something can be done to repel this raid on your immune system, and that something is the practice of advanced hygiene.

Proper hygiene supports your immune system in this constant battle against germs and foreign agents entering the body. I've been practicing an advanced hygiene regimen for more than a decade and have been the beneficiary of excellent health: no lingering head colds, no nagging sinus infections, and no acute respiratory illnesses to speak of for many years. I'm also confident that advanced hygiene is a superior *long-term weapon* against arthritis ever gaining a foothold within my body.

I urge you to follow the same program that I do. I begin each morning by standing before a sink and rubbing my hands in a creamy semisoft soap rich in essential oils. To properly wash my hands, I dip them into the tub of semisoft soap and dig my fingernails into the cream. Then I work the special cream around the tips of fingers, cuticles, and fingernails for fifteen to thirty seconds. When I'm finished, I lather my hands for fifteen seconds before rinsing them under running water. After my hands are clean, I take another dab of semisoft soap and wash my face.

I repeat this type of hand washing in the evening because I'm well aware that 90 percent of germs on my hands take up residence underneath my fingernails. If I've done a book signing and shaken a lot of hands or just gotten off a plane flight (where germs party like it's 1999), I'll do my best to wash my hands right away.

My second step involves a procedure that I call a facial dip. I fill my washbasin or a clean, large bowl with warm but not hot water. When enough water is in the basin, I add a tablespoon or two of regular table salt and two eyedroppers of a mineral-based facial solution to the cloudy water. I mix everything with my hands, and then I bend over and dip my face into the cleansing solution, opening my eyes several times to allow the membranes to be cleaned. After coming up for air, I dunk my head a second time and blow bubbles through my nose. "Sink snorkeling," I call it.

My final two steps of advanced hygiene involve applying very dilute drops of hydrogen peroxide and minerals into my ears for thirty to sixty seconds to cleanse the ear canal and then brushing my teeth with an essential oil–based tooth solution to cleanse my mouth of unhealthy germs.

Following this advanced hygiene protocol involves discipline; you have to remind yourself to do it until it becomes an ingrained habit. I find it easier to follow these steps in the morning and before bed. Since starting my hygiene regimen, I just don't feel clean without it. And the best part is, it takes less than three minutes from start to finish.

I urge you to incorporate advanced hygiene into your life, paying special attention to washing your hands periodically, especially after you've been in public situations and shaken the hands of a few friends. I don't want to drive up anyone's paranoia meter, but sometimes our biggest exposure to germs all week happens after church, when we're shaking hands with old friends and new acquaintances in the foyer. All the while, we're exchanging a garden variety of bacteria, allergens, environmental toxins, and viruses from one part of the body to another.

A Primer on Washing Your Hands

1. Wet your hands with warm water. It doesn't have to be anywhere near scalding hot.
2. Apply plenty of soap into the palms of both hands. The best soap to use is a semisoft soap that you can dig your fingernails into.
3. Rub your hands vigorously together and scrub all the surfaces. Pay attention to the skin between the fingers, and work the soap into the fingernails.
4. Rub and scrub for fifteen to thirty seconds, or about the time it takes to slowly sing "Happy Birthday."
5. Rinse well and dry your hands on a paper towel or clean cloth towel. If you're in a public restroom, it's a good idea to turn off the running water with the towel in your hand. An even *better* idea is to use that same towel to open the door since that door handle is the first place

that non-washers touch after they've gone to the bathroom.

6. Keep waterless sanitizers in your purse or wallet in case soap and water are not available in the public restroom. These towelettes, although not ideal, are better than nothing.

WHEN TO WASH YOUR HANDS

- After you go to the bathroom
- Before and after you insert and remove contact lenses
- Before and after food preparation
- Before you eat
- After you sneeze, cough, or blow your nose
- After cleaning up after your pet
- After handling money
- After changing a diaper
- After blowing a child's nose
- After handling garbage
- After cleaning your toilets
- After shaking hands with a bunch of people
- After shopping at the supermarket
- After attending an event at a public theater
- Before and after sexual intercourse

Rx THE GREAT PHYSICIAN'S RX FOR ARTHRITIS: PRACTICE ADVANCED HYGIENE

- *Wash your hands regularly, paying special attention to removing germs from underneath your fingernails.*
- *Cleanse your nasal passageways and the mucous membranes of the eyes daily by performing a facial dip.*
- *Cleanse the ear canals at least twice per week.*
- *Use an essential oil-based tooth solution daily to remove germs from the mouth and improve the health of the gums.*

Take Action

To learn how to incorporate the principles of practicing advanced hygiene into your daily lifestyle, please turn to page 74 for the Great Physician's Rx for Arthritis Battle Plan.

KEY #4

Condition Your Body with Exercise and Body Therapies

A blogger named Cloudmark on FoxSports.com decided to have a little fun at home-run hitter Barry Bonds's expense. What would it be like, he wondered, if we overheard the following phone conversation between Barry Bonds and his trainer, Greg Anderson?

BARRY BONDS: Dude, I need some more of that flaxseed oil for my arthritis.

GREG ANDERSON: Sure, Barry. I'll get you some more "flaxseed oil." Hey, wasn't that dinner great last night? That lobster was unbelievable.

BARRY BONDS: Lobster? I thought that was a tofu-based vitamin supplement formed into the shape of a shellfish, which tasted delicious and also helped me overcome my arthritis and fatigue. By the way, my arthritis was particularly bad since I had just played a day game right after a night game.

GREG ANDERSON: Good to hear. Hey, thanks for buying the dinner. I really enjoyed it.

BARRY BONDS: I never paid for your dinner, Greg. The reason I gave the waitress $600 was to thank you for

> the weight training we did last week. And that $20,000 in cash that I gave you was a bonus since I hit two home runs yesterday.[1]

I'm laughing like you, although my laughter has turned to tears. Five years ago, being the huge baseball fan that I am, I spent some coin on Barry Bonds memorabilia—a wall-sized original oil painting of the San Francisco slugger as well as a personally autographed bat and baseball. I thought Bonds memorabilia would explode in value, but then—if you've been following baseball at all the last couple of years—the market bottomed out after it became *very* apparent that Barry "juiced" his body with enough steroids to knock over an elephant.

It'll be interesting to see what Barry's health will be like in years to come, but these days he suffers from chronic osteoarthritis. The word is that he's worn out the cartilage in his right knee, and the bone-on-bone friction has prompted him to undergo three arthroscopic operations during his long career. This type of degenerative joint disease usually affects individuals when they are well into their fifties and sixties, but apparently Bonds's knees couldn't withstand the wear of 162-game seasons over the years.

If your knees aren't quite as bad as Barry's, a tailored exercise program can help relieve pain and fatigue associated with arthritic pain. Just because you have stiffness, swelling, and reduced range of motion in the joints, now is *not* the time to avoid physical activity. For many years, it was thought that those with arthritis shouldn't exercise because it would damage their joints, but doctors and therapists have shifted their point of view. Now they say that exercise, as part of a comprehensive arthritis treatment plan, can improve joint mobility, muscle strength, overall physical conditioning, and help you maintain a healthy weight.[2]

If you haven't darkened the door of a neighborhood fitness center in ages, or the last time you exercised was running after a foul ball at your son's Little League game, then let me introduce a great way to get back into the exercise game. It's called *functional fitness,* and this form of gentle exercise will be easy on your joints, get your body burning calories, and improve agility. The idea behind functional fitness is to train movements, not muscles, as you build up cardiovascular endurance and the body's core muscles. You do this through performing real-life activities in real-life positions.

Functional fitness employs your own body weight as resistance, but you can also utilize dumbbells, mini trampolines, and stability balls. Classes in functional fitness are gaining popularity around the country. Instructors at LA Fitness, Bally Total Fitness, and local YMCAs put you through a series of exercises that mimic everyday life. You're asked to perform squats with feet apart, feet together, and one back with the other forward. You're asked to do reaching lunges, push-ups against a wall, and "supermans" that involve lying on the floor and lifting up your right arm while lifting your left leg into a fully extended position. You're *not* asked to perform high-impact exercises like those found in energetic, pulsating aerobics classes. (For more information on functional fitness, visit www.BiblicalHealthInstitute.com.)

Your body's joints, cartilage, ligaments, muscles, bones, and tendons need to be used! Stretching and flexibility exercises, which are the core of functional fitness, help you maintain normal joint function by increasing and preserving joint mobility and flexibility. You can't stretch too much or too often when it comes to dealing with osteoarthritic knees and hips.

You should also incorporate some weight training into your regimen, which strengthens and develops muscle tissues. Stronger muscles help stabilize weak joints and protect them from further damage, all without aggravating your connective tissues. You should start out gradually when you begin "pushing plates" at your local health club and work your way to suit your comfort level.

Another great form of low-impact exercise is jumping on rebounders, which look like mini trampolines. One optimal rebound exercise session can cause a gentle but energized fatigue that revitalizes the lungs and the body's cells. According to my friend Morton Walker, DPM, author of *Jumping for Health,* each gentle bounce pits sixty trillion body cells against the earth's gravitational pull. This interaction strengthens every cell in the body while saving strain on its muscles and joints. The result, says Dr. Walker, is better health with less exertion.

WATER EXERCISE

A form of body therapy that's popular in the arthritis community is swimming laps or taking part in water aerobics classes. Aquatic exercise is tailor made for those with osteoarthritis because the water's buoyancy supports your weight. Standing in neck-deep water cancels out about 90 percent of your body weight, which greatly reduces stress on your weight-bearing joints.

Having an instructor lead you through a series of exercises may allow you to do certain movements that you can't do on land. Swimming laps certainly works the cardiovascular system and exercises muscles without jarring tender joints. A study at Flinders University in Australia, where swimming is big (as I learned during a visit to Down Under in 2006), pointed out that water-based exercise programs provide functional improvements for patients with osteoarthritis.[3]

While I'm all for water workouts, I must point out that 99 percent of pools these days are filled with chlorinated water. I'll be talking about environmental toxins like chlorine in the next chapter, but for now, let me say that I don't think it's very healthy to swim in pools with chlorine, a chemical compound used as a disinfectant to kill, destroy, or control bacteria and algae.

Chlorine is a fat-soluble chemical that is stored in our fatty tissues, where it takes months or years before this toxin is eliminated from our systems. The body treats it as a hostile foreign invader, which weakens our immune systems. If you're gung-ho to swim or perform aquatic exercises, try to find a saltwater pool.

Don't get me wrong—I think water can do a world of good for those dealing with painful arthritis. Baths, showers, steam rooms, saunas, washings, wraps, and hot tubs are forms of hydrotherapy, which is one of the easiest and cheapest ways to experience arthritis relief. Soaking in a tub of steamy hot water or standing under a strong spray of hot water facilitates muscle relaxation and decreases joint pain and stiffness, which makes joint movement easier. Hot water dilates blood vessels, which improves blood circulation and transports more oxygen to the brain.

If you're a bath type of person, then I recommend adding essential oils or herbs to the bath to enhance the therapeutic benefits. I also like Epsom salt baths because the high magnesium content facilitates the removal of acids through the skin. Although a potentially stinky experience, taking a warm bath with a cup of apple cider vinegar added can be great for the joints as well, provided you can handle the strong stench of vinegar.

You should also consider trying a brisk cold water shower for a minute or so, which stimulates the body and boosts oxygen use in the cells. Cold water—as well as applications of ice—reduces inflammation. Barry Bonds always ices his right knee after games, as do many professional athletes.

Even though I don't have arthritis, one of the healthy habits I do to *prevent* this chronic disease is alternating between hot water and cold water when I shower in the morning and evening. I warm up my body first with hot water, then slowly switch from hot to lukewarm to cool to as cold as I can stand it. Alternating between hot and cold water increases circulation of blood and lymphatic fluid.

Another great way to detoxify the body of harmful environmental chemicals, fat-soluble toxins, and heavy metals is the regular use of a far infrared sauna. Far infrared saunas improve health while gently raising the heart rate, and regular users have reported an improvement in skin tone and a lessening of aches and pains. I have owned and used a far infrared sauna for more than eight years and highly recommend it. (For more information on far infrared sauna technology, visit www.BiblicalHealthInstitute.com.)

For space reasons, I can't list all of my favorite body therapies, but I've mentioned a few below in the Great Physician's prescription pad.

℞ THE GREAT PHYSICIAN'S RX FOR ARTHRITIS: CONDITION YOUR BODY WITH EXERCISE AND BODY THERAPIES

- *Make a commitment and an appointment to exercise at least three times a week.*
- *Incorporate five to fifteen minutes of functional fitness into your daily schedule.*
- *Take a brisk walk and see how much better you feel at the end of the day.*
- *Make a conscious effort to practice deep-breathing exercises once a day. Sit in a chair and concentrate on filling the lungs completely. Inflate your lungs to full and hold for several seconds before slowly exhaling.*
- *Go to sleep earlier, paying close attention to how much sleep you get before midnight. Do your best to get eight hours of sleep nightly. Remember that sleep is the most important nonnutrient you can incorporate to improve your health.*

- *End your shower by changing the water temperature to cool (or cold) and standing underneath the spray for one minute.*

- *Each Saturday or Sunday, take a day of rest. Dedicate the day to the Lord and do something fun and relaxing that you haven't done in a while. Make your rest day work-free, errand-free, and shop-free. Trust God that He'll do more with His six days than you can do with seven.*

- *Once each day, sit outside in a chair and face the sun. Soak up the rays for ten or fifteen minutes, but do so before 10:00 a.m. and after 2:00 p.m.*

- *Play worship music in your home, in your car, or on your iPod. Focus on God's plan for your life.*

Take Action

To learn how to incorporate the principles of conditioning your body with exercise and body therapies into your daily lifestyle, please turn to page 74 for the Great Physician's Rx for Arthritis Battle Plan.

Key #5

Reduce Toxins in Your Environment

Modern medicine hasn't pinpointed the exact cause of arthritis, but researchers agree that your age, your weight, your family background, your athletic history, your occupation, and your diet are major risk factors. "We believe that osteoarthritis is not so much a single entity, but rather a family of disorders involving genetic and environmental factors," explained Farshid Guilak, Ph.D., director of orthopedic research at Duke University.[1]

I'm glad that Dr. Guilak mentioned the environmental component because I'm confident that toxins in our environment contribute to the development of osteoarthritis as people grow older. It's a physiological fact that when the immune system starts to go south, inflammation rates increase in the joint areas. It's another physiological fact that the body's immune systems are greatly impacted by toxins in our environment. A healthy immune system should reduce inflammation and pain.

Dr. Guilak is heading up a group of colleagues from Duke and the Durham VA Medical Center, and they are in the midst of a five-year, $7 million grant from the National Institute of Arthritis and Musculoskeletal and Skin Diseases (NIAMS), carrying out a broad range of laboratory experiments, as well as a clinical study. "Ten years ago, we didn't think the immune system was involved in osteoarthritis," said pain specialist Francis Keefe, Ph.D., co-principal investigator on the grant.[2]

Now they're taking a closer look. I'm glad that Duke University researchers are doing that because we all have toxins inside our bodies. Toxins are present everywhere in our environment—the air we breathe, the water we drink or swim in, the lotions and cosmetics we rub on our skin, the products we use to clean our homes, and even the toothpaste we dab on our toothbrushes. If your blood and urine were tested, lab technicians would uncover dozens of toxins in your bloodstream, including PCBs (polychlorinated biphenyls), dioxins, furans, trace metals, phthalates, VOCs (volatile organic compounds), and chlorine.

Some toxins are water soluble, meaning they are rapidly passed out of the body and present little harm. Unfortunately many more toxins are fat soluble, meaning that it can take months or years before they are completely eliminated from your system. I mentioned one of the better known fat-soluble toxins in my last chapter—chlorine. The best way to flush fat-soluble toxins like chlorine out of your bloodstream is to increase your intake of drinking water, which helps eliminate toxins through the kidneys (which I'll get into shortly).

Another way to reduce the number of toxins is to consume only organic or grass-fed meat and dairy products. Remember: most commercially produced beef, chicken, and pork act as chemical magnets for toxins in the environment, so they will not be as healthy as eating grass-fed beef or free-range chicken. In addition, consuming organic produce purchased at health food stores, roadside stands, and farmers' markets (only if produce is grown locally and unsprayed) will expose you to less pesticide residues, as compared to conventionally grown fruits and vegetables.

As I mentioned earlier, canned tuna, because of its high mercury levels, is another food to be careful of. Due to environmental contamination, metallic particles of mercury, lead, and aluminum continue to be found in the fatty tissues of certain fish, but you can find low mercury, high omega-3 tuna these days, which is an excellent animal protein. I recommend no more than two cans of tuna per week, however. Shrimp and lobster, which are shellfish that scavenge the ocean floor, are unclean meats that should be eliminated from your diet.

Drink to This

Those with arthritis tend to have sluggish livers because of toxic buildup in the body. When it comes to reducing toxins in your environment, drinking water throughout the day is especially important because of its ability to flush out toxins and other metabolic wastes from the body. Although I've already touted the healthy benefits of drinking water, it's good to be reminded that water is a life force involved in nearly every bodily process, from digestion to blood circulation. Your joints flex and move efficiently when you're well hydrated.

The answer to hydration is not switching to diet soft drinks or beverages such as coffee, tea, and fruit juice, even though the latter can be healthy for you. Diet drinks contain artificial sweeteners like aspartame, acesulfame K, or sucralose. Even though the Food and Drug Administration has approved the use of artificial sweeteners in drinks (and food), these chemical food additives may prove to be detrimental to your health in the long term.

Nothing beats plain old water—a liquid created by God to be totally compatible with your body. You should drink the proverbial eight glass of water daily.

I don't recommend drinking water straight from the tap, however. Nearly all municipal water is routinely treated with chlorine or chloramine, potent bacteria-killing chemicals. I've installed a whole-house filtration system that removes the chlorine and other impurities from the water *before* it enters our household pipes. My wife, Nicki, and I can confidently turn on the tap and enjoy the health benefits of chlorine-free water for drinking, cooking, and bathing. Since our water doesn't have a chemical aftertaste, we're more apt to drink it. Instead of installing a pricey whole-house filtration system, though, you can install an inexpensive water filter at your kitchen sink or purchase a countertop water pitcher with a built-in carbon-based filter.

Inside Our Homes

The American Lung Association estimates that we spend 90 percent of our time indoors, breathing recirculated air-conditioned air in the summer and heated air in the winter—air swirling with toxic particles. Today's well-insulated homes and energy-efficient doors and windows trap "used" air filled with carbon dioxide, nitrogen dioxide, and pet dander. These pollutants attack our immune systems relentlessly.

I recommend opening your doors and windows periodically to freshen the air you breathe, even if the temperatures are blazing hot or downright freezing. Just a few minutes of fresh air will do wonders. I also recommend the purchase of a quality air filter, which will remove and neutralize tiny airborne particles of dust, soot, pollen, mold, and dander. I have set up four high-quality air purifiers in our home that scrub harmful impurities out of the air.

TOXINS ELSEWHERE IN YOUR ENVIRONMENT

Other toxins not directly related to arthritis are important enough to mention:

- **Household cleaners.** Many of today's commercial house cleaners contain potentially harmful chemicals and solvents that expose people to VOCs—volatile organic compounds—that can cause eye, nose, and throat irritation. Nicki and I have found that natural ingredients like vinegar, lemon juice, and baking soda are excellent substances that make our home spick-and-span. Natural cleaning products that aren't harsh, abrasive, or potentially dangerous to your family are available in grocery and natural food stores.
- **Skin care and body care products.** Toxic chemicals such as chemical solvents and phthalates are found in lipstick, lip gloss, lip conditioner, hair coloring, hair spray, shampoo, and soap. Ladies, when you rub a tube of lipstick across your lips, your skin readily absorbs these toxins, and that's unhealthy. As with the case regarding household cleaners, you can find natural cosmetics in progressive natural food

markets, although they are becoming more widely available in drug stores and beauty stores.

- **Toothpaste.** A tube of toothpaste contains a warning that in case of accidental swallowing, you should contact the local Poison Control Center. What's that all about? Most commercially available toothpastes contain artificial sweeteners, potassium nitrate, sodium fluoride, and a whole bunch of long, unpronounceable words. Again, search out a healthy, natural version.

Let me leave you with this thought regarding toxins in your environment. As a defense, some scientists will quote Paracelsus, the famous medieval alchemist who said hundreds of years ago, "It's the dose that makes the poison." In other words, if the toxic dose is low enough, the body can handle it.

When I look at today's arthritis statistics, it's apparent that we are being hit with too many toxic doses from too many areas in our environment, and that's why we must be proactive in reducing toxins in our personal environments.

Rx THE GREAT PHYSICIAN'S RX FOR ARTHRITIS: REDUCE TOXINS IN YOUR ENVIRONMENT

- *Drink the recommended eight glasses of water daily—or one quart for every fifty pounds of body weight.*

- *Use glass containers instead of plastic containers whenever possible.*

- *Improve indoor air quality by opening windows and buying an air filtration system.*

- *Use natural cleaning products for your home.*

- *Use natural products for skin care, body care, hair care, cosmetics, and toothpaste.*

- *Don't smoke cigarettes or use tobacco products.*

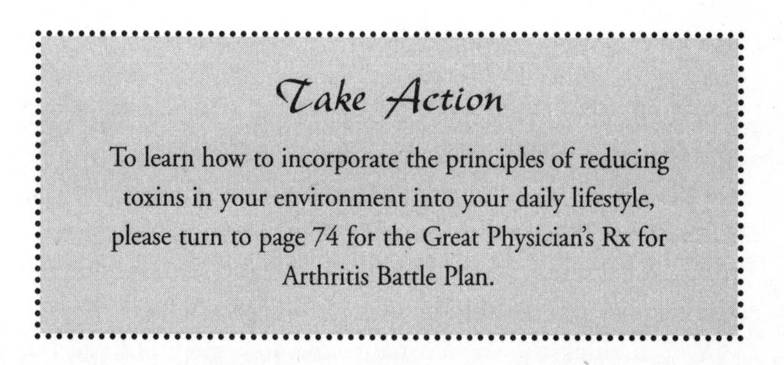

Take Action

To learn how to incorporate the principles of reducing toxins in your environment into your daily lifestyle, please turn to page 74 for the Great Physician's Rx for Arthritis Battle Plan.

KEY #6

Avoid Deadly Emotions

The chronic nature of constant arthritis pain can leave anyone feeling blue. Dealing with round-the-clock aches and throbbing soreness is a lot more than distressing: it can be downright depressing. Many with arthritis wonder if they will *ever* feel like their old selves.

Arthritis is not a life-threatening disease like cancer, but that doesn't lessen the impact of losing activities you once enjoyed or the freedom of movement you grew accustomed to. Some have to stop skiing, hitting tennis balls, or chasing a little white ball around a golf course. Others find hiking or even walking too much of a chore. No one feels chipper about facing an uncertain future with arthritis. If you're in this camp, then you know that your family life and career have been impacted by this chronic condition.

When it comes to the role of deadly emotions and arthritis, it boils down to the classic chicken-or-the-egg question: Which came first? Can someone who's depressed or angry start experiencing arthritic pain, or does arthritic pain cause depression and anger?

I don't think the answer matters because the mind and the body are linked. How you feel emotionally affects how you feel physically, and vice versa. What's noteworthy is that researchers, according to Don Colbert, M.D., author of *Deadly Emotions,* have directly and scientifically linked emotions to diseases related to the immune system, which would include arthritis.

If you're still bottling up emotions such as anger, bitterness, and resentment, these deadly emotions will produce toxins similar to bingeing on a dozen glazed doughnuts. The efficiency of your immune system decreases noticeably for six hours, which can raise inflammation levels in your joints and lay you down even lower. Staying angry and bitter about your bum knee or arthritic hip can alter the chemistry of your body—and even prompt you to fall off the healthy food wagon again. An old proverb states it well: "What you are eating is not nearly as important as what's eating you."

If you are in the midst of health challenges with steady arthritic pain, my heart goes out to you. It's beyond the scope of this book to delve deeper into the emotional pain that you may be enduring; for that, I urge you to speak with a counselor, your pastor, and trusted and loyal friends. Here I hope to remind you that deadly emotions can quickly deplete your dwindling reserves of energy and strength, especially if you are still dealing with depression and anger issues. "But a crushed spirit dries up the bones," notes the second half of Proverbs 17:22 (NIV)—and I bet the joints as well.

We've been talking about negative emotions and their effects on the body, but the flip side of the coin is that positive emotions such as love, acceptance, and laughter are a fragrant balm to the soul. "A cheerful heart is good medicine," declares the first half of Proverbs 17:22, and a jolt of humor could allow you to forget—at least momentarily—what's ailing you.

Norman Cousins, author of the best-selling *Anatomy of an Illness,* wrote about his discovery that ten minutes of solid belly laughter gave him two hours of pain-free sleep. "Since my illness involved severe inflammation of the spine and joints, making it painful even to turn over in bed, the practical value of laughter became a significant feature of treatment," he wrote. Cousins said he was gratified when the *Journal of the American Medical Association* (JAMA) published a study from Swedish medical researchers whose experiments showed that laughter helped the body to provide its own medication. "A humor therapy program can improve the quality of life for patients with chronic problems," said the report.[1]

If arthritis has you down, invite over some friends who always make you laugh. Watch something hilarious like Will Ferrell's side-splitting sketches from *Saturday Night Live* or riotous reruns of *I Love Lucy*.

One of the deadliest of all emotions is unforgiveness that turns to bitterness. Are there people in your life who've done you a great injustice—or bug you so much—that you can't find it in your heart to forgive them? It's a question worth pondering because I believe an unforgiving heart is an underlying factor in many health problems, including chronic, incurable illnesses like arthritis.

Please remember that no matter how bad you've been hurt in the past, it's still possible to forgive. Jesus said, "For if you forgive men their trespasses, your heavenly Father will also forgive you. But if you don't forgive men their trespasses, neither will your Father forgive your trespasses" (Matt. 6:14–15 NKJV).

If you're angry, hurt, or bothered by those who've been mean to you, give them your forgiveness, and then let it go.

Rx THE GREAT PHYSICIAN'S RX FOR ARTHRITIS: AVOID DEADLY EMOTIONS

- *Simplify your life and do your best to avoid stress, anxiety, and anger.*
- *Trust God when you face circumstances that cause you to worry or become anxious.*
- *Look for ways to laugh; it's your best medicine (Prov. 17:22).*

Take Action

To learn how to incorporate the principles of avoiding deadly emotions into your daily lifestyle, please turn to page 74 for the Great Physician's Rx for Arthritis Battle Plan.

Key #7

Live a Life of Prayer and Purpose

If you or a loved one has been afflicted by arthritis, I would imagine that you've been driven to your knees in prayer. (I hope those arthritic joints are okay.) There's something about this painful affliction—which has no known medical cure—that causes one to plead for healing from the One who "fearfully and wonderfully made" us (Ps. 139:14 NKJV).

I believe that God is still in the healing business, and He listens to each and every prayer that we direct His way. Prayer is the foundation of a healthy life, linking your mind, body, and spirit to God. Prayer is two-way communication with our Creator, the God of the universe. There's power in prayer: "The prayer offered in faith will make the sick person well" (James 5:15 NIV).

Prayer is how we talk to God. There is no greater source of power than talking to the One who made us. Prayer is not a formality. Prayer is not about religion. Prayer is about a relationship—the hotline to heaven. We can talk to God anytime, anywhere, for any reason. He is always there to listen, and He always has our best interests at heart because we are His children.

In living a healthy, purpose-filled life, prayer is the most powerful tool that we possess. Prayer connects the entire person—body, mind, and spirit—to God. Through prayer, God takes away our guilt, shame, bitterness, and anger and gives us a brand-new start. We can eat organic whole foods, supplement our diet with whole food supplements, practice advanced hygiene, reduce toxins, and exercise, but if the spirit is not where it needs to be with God, then we will never be completely healthy. Talking to our Maker through prayer is the foundation for optimal health and makes us whole. After all, God's love and grace are our greatest foods for mind, body, and spirit.

The seventh key to unlocking your health potential is living a life of prayer and purpose. Prayer will confirm your purpose, and it will give you the perseverance to complete it. Seal all that you do with the power of prayer, and watch your life become more than you ever thought possible.

Finding His Purpose

"Living a life of purpose" is a buzz phrase these days because of a certain book you've probably read or heard about—*The Purpose-Driven Life* by Rick Warren, pastor of Saddleback Church in Lake Forest, California.

When God took Pat McCleave through years of painful gout before restoring his health, he came out of that experience knowing what his purpose was in life: to get healthy so that he could be the best father to his children and the best husband to his wife, Tammy. "I have a fourteen-year-old son and an eleven-year-old daughter who need a father," Pat said. "I need to walk my daughter down the aisle one day. I have a brother and sister who count on me to be there, and they have families."

Does Pat feel that he's been given a second chance on life? "I wouldn't go that far, but my life has changed. My whole overall attitude is better. I still have some personal and spiritual issues to work through, but I think everyone tries to work through those. I tell you this, though: the Great Physician's prescription has made life easier and given me a purpose."

If you say to yourself, *I'm not sure I have a purpose,* you would be wrong. If there is breath in your lungs, you have a purpose; it's ingrained in your being. If you haven't found your purpose yet, search your heart. What makes you feel alive? What are you passionate about? The joys of family? The arts? Teaching others? Your purpose is waiting to be discovered. Pinpoint your passions, and you'll uncover your purpose. Keep in mind that God gives us different desires, dreams, and talents for a reason because we are all part of one body. Having a purpose will give you something to live for.

Don't let arthritis keep you down. You can bounce back. I urge you to follow the Great Physician's prescription today. I've yet to meet anyone who regretted feeling better and becoming healthier, and you won't either.

Start a Small Group

It's difficult to face arthritis alone. If you have friends or family members struggling with similar symptoms, ask them to join you in following the Great Physician's Rx 7 Weeks of Wellness small group curriculum. To learn about joining an existing group in the area or leading a small group in your church, please visit www.BiblicalHealthInstitute.com.

℞ THE GREAT PHYSICIAN'S RX FOR ARTHRITIS: LIVE A LIFE OF PRAYER AND PURPOSE

- *Pray continually.*
- *Confess God's promises upon waking and before you retire.*
- *Find God's purpose for your life and live it.*
- *Be an agent of change in your life by adopting the seven keys into your life.*

Take Action

To learn how to incorporate the principles of living a life of prayer and purpose into your daily lifestyle, please turn to page 74 for the Great Physician's Rx for Arthritis Battle Plan.

The Great Physician's Rx for Arthritis Battle Plan

Day 1

Upon Waking

Prayer: thank God because this is the day that the Lord has made. Rejoice and be glad in it. Thank Him for the breath in your lungs and the life in your body. Ask the Lord to heal your body and use your experience to benefit the lives of others. Read Matthew 6:9–13 aloud.

Purpose: ask the Lord to give you an opportunity to add significance to someone's life today. Watch for that opportunity. Ask God to use you this day for His intended purpose.

Advanced hygiene: for hands and nails, jab fingers into semisoft soap four or five times, and lather hands with soap for fifteen seconds, rubbing soap over cuticles and rinsing under water as warm as you can stand. Take another swab of semisoft soap into your hands and wash your face. Next, fill basin or sink with water as warm as you can stand, and add one to three tablespoons of table salt and one to three eyedroppers of iodine-based mineral solution. Dunk face into water and open eyes, blinking repeatedly underwater. Keep eyes open underwater for three seconds. After cleaning your eyes, put your face back in the water, and close your mouth while blowing bubbles out of your nose. Come up from the water, and immerse your face in the water once again, gently taking water into your nostrils and expelling bubbles. Come up from the water, and blow your nose into facial tissue. To cleanse the ears, use hydrogen peroxide and mineral-based ear drops, putting two or three drops into each ear and letting it stand for sixty seconds. Tilt your head to expel the drops. For the teeth, apply two or three drops of essential oil–based tooth drops to the toothbrush. This can be used to brush your teeth or added to existing toothpaste. After brushing your teeth, brush your tongue for fifteen seconds. (For recommended advanced hygiene products, visit www.BiblicalHealthInstitute.com and click on the Resource Guide.)

Reduce toxins: open your windows for one hour today. Use natural soap and natural skin and body care products (shower gel, body creams, etc.). Use natural facial care products. Use natural toothpaste. Use natural hair care products such as shampoo, conditioner, gel, mousse, and hairspray. (For recommended products, visit www.BiblicalHealthInstitute.com and click on the Resource Guide.)

Supplements: make a drink with one tablespoon of organic raw apple cider vinegar and two teaspoons of raw organic honey dissolved in twelve ounces of warm purified water. Drink while taking two capsules of a systemic enzyme blend with proteases, bromelain, and papain. (For recommended products, visit www.BiblicalHealthInstitute.com and click on the Resource Guide.)

Body therapy: get twenty minutes of direct sunlight sometime during the day, but be careful between the hours of 10:00 a.m. and 2:00 p.m.

Exercise: perform functional fitness exercises for five to fifteen minutes or spend five to fifteen minutes on a mini trampoline. Finish with five to ten minutes of deep-breathing exercises. (One to three rounds of the exercises can be found at www.BiblicalHealthInstitute.com.)

Emotional health: whenever you face a circumstance, such as your health, that causes you to worry, repeat the following: "Lord, I trust You. I cast my cares upon You, and I believe that You're going to take care of [insert your current situation] and make my health and my body strong." Confess that throughout the day whenever you think about your health condition.

Breakfast

Make a smoothie in a blender with the following ingredients:

1 cup organic plain yogurt or kefir (goat's milk is best)

1 tablespoon organic flaxseed oil

1 to 2 tablespoons organic raw honey

1 cup organic fruit (berries, banana, peaches, pineapple, etc.)

2 tablespoons goat's milk protein powder (for recommended brands, visit www.BiblicalHealthInstitute.com and click on the Resource Guide)

dash of vanilla extract (optional)

Supplements: take two whole food multivitamin caplets and two capsules of a natural non-shellfish glucosamine product with *Boswellia serrata,* ginger, and turmeric. (For recommended brands, visit www.BiblicalHealthInstitute.com and click on the Resource Guide.)

Lunch

Before eating, drink eight ounces of water.

During lunch, drink eight ounces of water or hot or iced green tea with honey.

large green salad with mixed greens, avocado, carrots, tomato, red cabbage, red onions, red peppers, and sprouts with three hard-boiled omega-3 eggs

salad dressing: mix extra virgin olive oil, apple cider vinegar or lemon juice, minced fresh garlic, naturally brewed soy sauce, Celtic Sea Salt, herbs, and spices; or, mix one tablespoon of extra virgin olive oil with one tablespoon of a healthy store-bought dressing

one apple with skin

Supplements: take two whole food multivitamin caplets and two capsules of a natural non-shellfish glucosamine product with *Boswellia serrata,* ginger, and turmeric.

Dinner

Before eating, drink eight ounces of water.

During dinner, drink hot or iced green tea with honey (for recommended brands, visit www.BiblicalHealthInstitute.com and click on the Resource Guide).

baked, poached, or grilled wild-caught salmon

steamed broccoli

large green salad with mixed greens, avocado, carrots, cucumbers, celery, tomato, red cabbage, red onions, red peppers, and sprouts

salad dressing: mix extra virgin olive oil, apple cider vinegar or lemon juice, minced fresh garlic, naturally brewed soy sauce, Celtic Sea Salt, herbs, and spices; or, mix one tablespoon of extra virgin olive oil with one tablespoon of a healthy store-bought dressing

Supplements: take two whole food multivitamin caplets and two capsules of a natural non-shellfish glucosamine product with *Boswellia serrata,* ginger, and turmeric as well as one to three teaspoons or three to nine capsules of a high omega-3 cod-liver oil complex. (For recommended brands, visit www.BiblicalHealthInstitute.com and click on the Resource Guide.)

Snacks

apple slices with raw almond butter

one berry antioxidant whole food nutrition bar with beta-glucans from soluble oat fiber (for recommended brands, visit www.BiblicalHealthInstitute.com and click on the Resource Guide)

eight to twelve ounces of water, or hot or iced green tea with honey (for recommended brands, visit www.BiblicalHealthInstitute.com and click on the Resource Guide)

Before Bed

Exercise: go for a walk outdoors or participate in a favorite sport or recreational activity.

Supplements: make a drink with one tablespoon of organic raw apple cider vinegar and two teaspoons of raw organic honey dissolved in twelve ounces of warm purified water. Drink while taking two capsules of a systemic enzyme blend with proteases, bromelain, and papain. (For recommended products, visit www.BiblicalHealthInstitute.com and click on the Resource Guide.)

Body therapy: take a warm bath for fifteen minutes with eight drops of biblical essential oils added.

Advanced hygiene: repeat the advanced hygiene instructions from the morning of Day 1.

Emotional health: ask the Lord to bring to your mind someone you need to forgive. Take a sheet of paper and write the person's name at the top. Try to remember each specific action that person did that brought you pain. Write the following: "I forgive [insert person's name] for [insert the action he or she did]." After you fill up the paper, tear it up or burn it, and ask God to give you the strength to truly forgive that person.

Purpose: ask yourself these questions: "Did I live a life of purpose today?" "What did I do to add value to someone else's life today?" Commit to living a day of purpose tomorrow.

Prayer: thank God for this day, asking Him to give you a restoring night's rest and a fresh start tomorrow. Thank Him for His steadfast love that never ceases and His mercies that are new every morning. Read Romans 8:35, 37–39 aloud.

Sleep: go to bed by 10:30 p.m.

DAY 2

Upon Waking

Prayer: thank God because this is the day that the Lord has made. Rejoice and be glad in it. Thank Him for the breath in your lungs and the life in your body. Ask the Lord to heal your body and use your experience to benefit the lives of others. Read Psalm 91 aloud.

Purpose: ask the Lord to give you an opportunity to add significance to someone's life today. Watch for that opportunity. Ask God to use you this day for His intended purpose.

Advanced hygiene: follow the advanced hygiene recommendations from the morning of Day 1.

Reduce toxins: follow the recommendations to reduce toxins from the morning of Day 1.

Supplements: make a drink with one tablespoon of organic raw apple cider vinegar and two teaspoons of raw organic honey dissolved in twelve ounces of warm purified water. Drink while taking two capsules of a systemic enzyme blend with proteases, bromelain, and papain. (For recommended products, visit www.BiblicalHealthInstitute.com and click on the Resource Guide.)

Body therapy: take a hot and cold shower. After a normal shower, alternate sixty seconds of water as hot as you can stand it, followed by sixty seconds of water as cold as you can stand it. Repeat cycle four times for a total of eight minutes, finishing with cold.

Exercise: perform functional fitness exercises for five to fifteen minutes or spend five to fifteen minutes on a mini trampoline. Finish with five to ten minutes of deep-breathing exercises. (One to three rounds of the exercises can be found at www.BiblicalHealthInstitute.com.)

Emotional health: follow the emotional health recommendations from the morning of Day 1.

Breakfast

two or three omega-3 eggs any style, cooked in one tablespoon of extra virgin coconut oil (for recommended brands, visit www.Biblical HealthInstitute.com and click on the Resource Guide)

stir-fried onions, garlic, mushrooms, and peppers

one slice of sprouted or yeast-free whole grain bread with almond butter and honey

Supplements: take two whole food multivitamin caplets and two capsules of a natural non-shellfish glucosamine product with *Boswellia serrata,* ginger, and turmeric.

Lunch

Before eating, drink eight ounces of water.

During lunch, drink eight ounces of water or hot or iced green tea with honey.

large green salad with mixed greens, avocado, carrots, tomato, red cabbage, red onions, red peppers, and sprouts with two ounces of low mercury, high omega-3 tuna (for recommended brands, visit www.BiblicalHealthInstitute.com and click on the Resource Guide)

salad dressing: mix extra virgin olive oil, apple cider vinegar or lemon juice, minced fresh garlic, naturally brewed soy sauce, Celtic Sea Salt, herbs, and spices; or, mix one tablespoon of extra virgin olive oil with one tablespoon of a healthy store-bought dressing

organic dark grapes (preferably with seeds)

Supplements: take two whole food multivitamin caplets and two capsules of a natural non-shellfish glucosamine product with *Boswellia serrata,* ginger, and turmeric.

Dinner

Before eating, drink eight ounces of water.

During dinner, drink hot or iced green tea with honey.

roasted organic chicken

cooked vegetables (carrots, onions, garlic, peas, etc.)

large green salad with mixed greens, avocado, carrots, tomato, red cabbage, red onions, red peppers, and sprouts

salad dressing: mix extra virgin olive oil, apple cider vinegar or lemon juice, minced fresh garlic, naturally brewed soy sauce, Celtic Sea Salt, herbs, and spices; or, mix one tablespoon of extra virgin olive oil with one tablespoon of a healthy store-bought dressing

Supplements: take two whole food multivitamin caplets and two capsules of a natural non-shellfish glucosamine product with *Boswellia*

serrata, ginger, and turmeric with one to three teaspoons or three to nine capsules of a high omega-3 cod-liver oil complex.

Snacks

one cup of organic berries

one berry antioxidant whole food nutrition bar with beta-glucans from soluble oat fiber

eight to twelve ounces of water or hot or iced green tea with honey

Before Bed

Exercise: go for a walk outdoors or participate in a favorite sport or recreational activity.

Supplements: make a drink with one tablespoon of organic raw apple cider vinegar and two teaspoons of raw organic honey dissolved in twelve ounces of warm purified water. Drink while taking two capsules of a systemic enzyme blend with proteases, bromelain, and papain. (For recommended products, visit www.BiblicalHealthInstitute.com and click on the Resource Guide.)

Advanced hygiene: repeat the advanced hygiene instructions from the morning of Day 1.

Emotional health: repeat the emotional health recommendations from Day 1.

Purpose: ask yourself these questions: "Did I live a life of purpose today?" "What did I do to add value to someone else's life today?" Commit to living a day of purpose tomorrow.

Prayer: thank God for this day, asking Him to give you a restoring night's rest and a fresh start tomorrow. Thank Him for His steadfast love that never ceases and His mercies that are new every morning. Read 1 Corinthians 13:4–8 aloud.

Body therapy: spend ten minutes listening to soothing music before you retire.

Sleep: go to bed by 10:30 p.m.

DAY 3

Upon Waking

Prayer: thank God because this is the day that the Lord has made. Rejoice and be glad in it. Thank Him for the breath in your lungs and the life in your body. Ask the Lord to heal your body and use your experience to benefit the lives of others. Read Ephesians 6:13–18 aloud.

Purpose: ask the Lord to give you an opportunity to add significance to someone's life today. Watch for that opportunity. Ask God to use you this day for His intended purpose.

Advanced hygiene: follow the advanced hygiene recommendations from the morning of Day 1.

Reduce toxins: follow the recommendations to reduce toxins from the morning of Day 1.

Supplements: make a drink with one tablespoon of organic raw apple cider vinegar and two teaspoons of raw organic honey dissolved in twelve ounces of warm purified water. Drink while taking two capsules of a systemic enzyme blend with proteases, bromelain, and papain. (For recommended products, visit www.BiblicalHealthInstitute.com and click on the Resource Guide.)

Body therapy: get twenty minutes of direct sunlight sometime during the day, but be careful between the hours of 10:00 a.m. and 2:00 p.m.

Exercise: perform functional fitness exercises for five to fifteen minutes or spend five to fifteen minutes on a mini trampoline. Finish with five to ten minutes of deep-breathing exercises. (One to three rounds of the exercises can be found at www.BiblicalHealthInstitute.com.)

Emotional health: follow the emotional health recommendations from Day 1.

Breakfast

four to eight ounces of organic whole milk yogurt or cottage cheese with fruit (pineapple, peaches, or berries), one teaspoon of raw organic honey, one teaspoon of flaxseed oil, and a dash of vanilla extract

handful of raw almonds

one cup of hot or iced green tea with honey

Supplements: take two whole food multivitamin caplets and two capsules of a natural non-shellfish glucosamine product with *Boswellia serrata,* ginger, and turmeric.

Lunch

Before eating, drink eight ounces of water.

During lunch, drink eight ounces of water or hot or iced green tea with honey.

large green salad with mixed greens, avocado, carrots, tomato, red cabbage, red onions, red peppers, and sprouts with three hard-boiled omega-3 eggs

salad dressing: mix extra virgin olive oil, apple cider vinegar or lemon juice, minced fresh garlic, naturally brewed soy sauce, Celtic Sea Salt, herbs, and spices; or, mix one tablespoon of extra virgin olive oil with one tablespoon of a healthy store-bought dressing

organic grapes or berries

Supplements: take two whole food multivitamin caplets and two capsules of a natural non-shellfish glucosamine product with *Boswellia serrata,* ginger, and turmeric.

Dinner

Before eating, drink eight ounces of water.

During dinner, drink hot or iced green tea with honey.

red meat steak (beef, buffalo, or venison)

steamed broccoli

baked sweet potato with butter

large green salad with mixed greens, avocado, carrots, tomato, red cabbage, red onions, red peppers, and sprouts salad dressing: mix extra virgin olive oil, apple cider vinegar or lemon juice, minced fresh garlic, naturally brewed soy sauce, Celtic Sea Salt, herbs, and spices; or, mix one tablespoon of extra virgin olive oil with one tablespoon of a healthy store-bought dressing

Supplements: take two whole food multivitamin caplets and two capsules of a natural non-shellfish glucosamine product with *Boswellia serrata,* ginger, and turmeric with one to three teaspoons or three to nine capsules of a high omega-3 cod-liver oil complex.

Snacks

healthy chocolate (cacao) snack (for recommended brands, visit www.BiblicalHealthInstitute.com and click on the Resource Guide)

one whole food nutrition bar with beta-glucans from soluble oat fiber

eight to twelve ounces of water or hot or iced green tea with honey

Before Bed

Exercise: go for a walk outdoors or participate in a favorite sport or recreational activity.

Supplements: make a drink with one tablespoon of organic raw apple cider vinegar and two teaspoons of raw organic honey dissolved in twelve ounces of warm purified water. Drink while taking two capsules of a systemic enzyme blend with proteases, bromelain, and papain. (For recommended products, visit www.BiblicalHealthInstitute.com and click on the Resource Guide.)

Body therapy: take a warm bath for fifteen minutes with eight drops of biblical essential oils added.

Advanced hygiene: follow the advanced hygiene instructions from the morning of Day 1.

Emotional health: follow the forgiveness recommendations from the evening of Day 1.

Purpose: ask yourself these questions: "Did I live a life of purpose today?" "What did I do to add value to someone else's life today?" Commit to living a day of purpose tomorrow.

Prayer: thank God for this day, asking Him to give you a restoring night's rest and a fresh start tomorrow. Thank Him for His steadfast love that never ceases and His mercies that are new every morning. Read Philippians 4:4–8, 11–13, 19 aloud.

Sleep: go to bed by 10:30 p.m.

DAY 4

Upon Waking

Prayer: thank God because this is the day that the Lord has made. Rejoice and be glad in it. Thank Him for the breath in your lungs and the life in your body. Read Matthew 6:9–13 out loud.

Purpose: ask the Lord to give you an opportunity to add significance to someone's life today. Watch for that opportunity. Ask God to use you this day for His intended purpose.

Advanced hygiene: follow the advanced hygiene recommendations from Day 1.

Reduce toxins: follow the recommendations for reducing toxins from Day 1.

Supplements: make a drink with one tablespoon of organic raw apple cider vinegar and two teaspoons of raw organic honey dissolved in twelve ounces of warm purified water. Drink while taking two capsules of a systemic enzyme blend with proteases, bromelain, and papain. (For recommended products, visit www.BiblicalHealthInstitute.com and click on the Resource Guide.)

Exercise: perform functional fitness exercises for five to fifteen minutes or spend five to fifteen minutes on a mini trampoline. Finish with five to ten minutes of deep-breathing exercises. (One to three rounds of the exercises can be found at www.BiblicalHealthInstitute.com.)

Body therapy: take a hot and cold shower. After a normal shower, alternate sixty seconds of water as hot as you can stand it, followed by sixty seconds of water as cold as you can stand it. Repeat cycle four times for a total of eight minutes, finishing with cold.

Emotional health: follow the emotional health recommendations from the morning of Day 1.

Breakfast

three soft-boiled or poached omega-3 eggs

four ounces of sprouted whole grain cereal with two ounces of whole milk yogurt or goat's milk (for recommended brands, visit www.BiblicalHealthInstitute.com and click on the Resource Guide)

one cup of hot or iced green tea with honey

Supplements: take two whole food multivitamin caplets and two capsules of a natural non-shellfish glucosamine product with *Boswellia serrata,* ginger, and turmeric.

Lunch

Before eating, drink eight ounces of water.

During lunch, drink eight ounces of water or hot green tea with honey.

large green salad with mixed greens, avocado, carrots, tomato, red cabbage, red onions, red peppers, and sprouts with two ounces of low mercury, high omega-3 tuna (for recommended brands, visit www.BiblicalHealthInstitute.com and click on the Resource Guide)

salad dressing: mix extra virgin olive oil, apple cider vinegar or lemon juice, minced fresh garlic, naturally brewed soy sauce, Celtic Sea Salt, herbs, and spices; or, mix one tablespoon of extra virgin olive oil with one tablespoon of a healthy store-bought dressing

one bunch of organic dark grapes (preferably with seeds)

Supplements: take two whole food multivitamin caplets and two capsules of a natural non-shellfish glucosamine product with *Boswellia serrata,* ginger, and turmeric. (For recommended brands, visit www.BiblicalHealthInstitute.com and click on the Resource Guide.)

Dinner

Before eating, drink eight ounces of water.

During dinner, drink hot green tea with honey.

grilled chicken breast

steamed veggies

small portion of cooked whole grain (quinoa, amaranth, millet, or brown rice) cooked with one tablespoon of extra virgin coconut oil

large green salad with mixed greens, avocado, carrots, tomato, red cabbage, red onions, red peppers, and sprouts

salad dressing: mix extra virgin olive oil, apple cider vinegar or lemon juice, minced fresh garlic, naturally brewed soy sauce, Celtic Sea Salt, herbs, and spices; or, mix one tablespoon of extra virgin olive oil with one tablespoon of a healthy store-bought dressing

Supplements: take two whole food multivitamin caplets and two capsules of a natural non-shellfish glucosamine product with *Boswellia serrata,* ginger, and turmeric with one to three teaspoons or three to nine capsules of a high omega-3 cod-liver oil complex.

Snacks

apple and carrots with raw almond butter

one berry antioxidant whole food nutrition bar with beta-glucans from soluble oat fiber

eight to twelve ounces of water or hot or iced green tea with honey

Before Bed

Drink eight to twelve ounces of water or hot or iced green tea with honey.

Exercise: go for a walk outdoors or participate in a favorite sport or recreational activity.

Supplements: make a drink with one tablespoon of organic raw apple cider vinegar and two teaspoons of raw organic honey dissolved in twelve ounces of warm purified water. Drink while taking two capsules of a systemic enzyme blend with proteases, bromelain, and papain. (For recommended products, visit www.BiblicalHealthInstitute.com and click on the Resource Guide.)

Advanced hygiene: follow the advanced hygiene recommendations from the morning of Day 1.

Emotional health: follow the forgiveness recommendations from the evening of Day 1.

Purpose: ask yourself these questions: "Did I live a life of purpose today?" "What did I do to add value to someone else's life today?" Commit to living a day of purpose tomorrow.

Prayer: thank God for this day, asking Him to give you a restoring night's rest and a fresh start tomorrow. Thank Him for His steadfast love that never ceases and His mercies that are new every morning. Read Romans 8:35, 37–39 aloud.

Body therapy: spend ten minutes listening to soothing music before you retire.

Sleep: go to bed by 10:30 p.m.

DAY 5 (PARTIAL FAST DAY)

Upon Waking

Prayer: thank God because this is the day that the Lord has made. Rejoice and be glad in it. Thank Him for the breath in your lungs and the life in your body. Read Isaiah 58:6–9 aloud.

Purpose: ask the Lord to give you an opportunity to add significance to someone's life today. Watch for that opportunity. Ask God to use you this day for His intended purpose.

Advanced hygiene: follow the advanced hygiene recommendations from Day 1.

Reduce toxins: follow the recommendations for reducing toxins from Day 1.

Supplements: make a drink with one tablespoon of organic raw apple cider vinegar and two teaspoons of raw organic honey dissolved in twelve ounces of warm purified water. Drink while taking two capsules of a systemic enzyme blend with proteases, bromelain, and papain. (For recommended products, visit www.BiblicalHealthInstitute.com and click on the Resource Guide.)

Exercise: perform functional fitness exercises for five to fifteen minutes or spend five to fifteen minutes on a mini trampoline. Finish with five to ten minutes of deep-breathing exercises.

Body therapy: get twenty minutes of direct sunlight sometime during the day, but be careful between the hours of 10:00 a.m. and 2:00 p.m.

Emotional health: follow the emotional health recommendations from the morning of Day 1.

Breakfast

none (partial fast day)

Drink eight to twelve ounces of water.

Lunch

none (partial fast day)

Drink eight to twelve ounces of water.

Dinner

Before eating, drink eight ounces of water.

During dinner, drink hot or iced green tea with honey.

chicken soup (visit www.BiblicalHealthInstitute.com for the recipe)

cultured vegetables (for recommended brands, visit www.BiblicalHealthInstitute.com and click on the Resource Guide)

large green salad with mixed greens, avocado, carrots, tomato, red cabbage, red onions, red peppers, and sprouts

salad dressing: mix extra virgin olive oil, apple cider vinegar or lemon juice, minced fresh garlic, naturally brewed soy sauce, Celtic Sea Salt, herbs, and spices; or, mix one tablespoon of extra virgin olive oil with one tablespoon of a healthy store-bought dressing

Supplements: take two whole food multivitamin caplets and two capsules of a natural non-shellfish glucosamine product with *Boswellia serrata,* ginger, and turmeric with one to three teaspoons or three to nine capsules of a high omega-3 cod-liver oil complex.

Snacks

none (partial fast day)

eight to twelve ounces of water

Before Bed

Drink eight to twelve ounces of water or hot or iced green tea with honey.

Exercise: go for a walk outdoors or participate in a favorite sport or recreational activity.

Supplements: make a drink with one tablespoon of organic raw apple cider vinegar and two teaspoons of raw organic honey dissolved in twelve ounces of warm purified water. Drink while taking two capsules of a systemic enzyme blend with proteases, bromelain, and papain. (For recommended products, visit www.BiblicalHealthInstitute.com and click on the Resource Guide.)

Advanced hygiene: follow the advanced hygiene recommendations from the morning of Day 1.

Emotional health: follow the forgiveness recommendations from the evening of Day 1.

Body therapy: take a warm bath for fifteen minutes with eight drops of biblical essential oils added.

Purpose: ask yourself these questions: "Did I live a life of purpose today?" "What did I do to add value to someone else's life today?" Commit to living a day of purpose tomorrow.

Prayer: thank God for this day, asking Him to give you a restoring night's rest and a fresh start tomorrow. Thank Him for His steadfast love that never ceases and His mercies that are new every morning. Read Isaiah 58:6–9 aloud.

Sleep: go to bed by 10:30 p.m.

DAY 6 (REST DAY)

Upon Waking

Prayer: thank God because this is the day that the Lord has made. Rejoice and be glad in it. Thank Him for the breath in your lungs and the life in your body. Read Psalm 23 aloud.

Purpose: ask the Lord to give you an opportunity to add significance to someone's life today. Watch for that opportunity. Ask God to use you this day for His intended purpose.

Advanced hygiene: follow the advanced hygiene recommendations from Day 1.

Reduce toxins: follow the recommendations for reducing toxins from Day 1.

Supplements: make a drink with one tablespoon of organic raw apple cider vinegar and two teaspoons of raw organic honey dissolved in twelve ounces of warm purified water. Drink while taking two capsules of a systemic enzyme blend with proteases, bromelain, and papain. (For recommended products, visit www.BiblicalHealthInstitute.com and click on the Resource Guide.)

Exercise: no formal exercise since it's a rest day.

Body therapies: none since it's a rest day.

Emotional health: follow the emotional health recommendations from the morning of Day 1.

Breakfast

one cup of hot or iced green tea with honey

two or three omega-3 eggs cooked any style in one tablespoon of extra virgin coconut oil

two ounces of smoked wild salmon

one grapefruit or orange

handful of almonds

Supplements: take two whole food multivitamin caplets and two capsules of a natural non-shellfish glucosamine product with *Boswellia serrata,* ginger, and turmeric. (For recommended brands, visit www.BiblicalHealthInstitute.com and click on the Resource Guide.)

Lunch

Before eating, drink eight ounces of water.

During lunch, drink eight ounces of water or hot or iced green tea with honey.

large green salad with mixed greens, avocado, carrots, cucumbers, celery, tomatoes, red cabbage, red peppers, red onions, and sprouts with two ounces of low mercury, high omega-3 tuna

salad dressing: mix extra virgin olive oil, apple cider vinegar or lemon juice, minced fresh garlic, naturally brewed soy sauce, Celtic Sea Salt, herbs, and spices; or, mix one tablespoon of extra virgin olive oil with one tablespoon of a healthy store-bought dressing one organic apple with the skin

Supplements: take two whole food multivitamin caplets and two capsules of a natural non-shellfish glucosamine product with *Boswellia serrata,* ginger, and turmeric.

Dinner

Before eating, drink eight ounces of water.

During dinner, drink hot or iced green tea with honey.

roasted organic chicken

cooked vegetables (carrots, onions, peas, etc.)

large green salad with mixed greens, avocado, carrots, tomato, red cabbage, red onions, red peppers, and sprouts

salad dressing: mix extra virgin olive oil, apple cider vinegar or lemon juice, minced fresh garlic, naturally brewed soy sauce, Celtic Sea Salt, herbs, and spices; or, mix one tablespoon of extra virgin olive oil with one tablespoon of a healthy store-bought dressing

Supplements: take two whole food multivitamin caplets and two capsules of a natural non-shellfish glucosamine product with *Boswellia serrata,* ginger, and turmeric with one to three teaspoons or three to nine capsules of a high omega-3 cod-liver oil complex.

Snacks

one serving of high antioxidant berry powder with beta-glucans from soluble oat fiber mixed in eight to twelve ounces of water (for recommended brands, visit www.BiblicalHealthInstitute.com and click on the Resource Guide)

one berry antioxidant whole food nutrition bar with beta-glucans from soluble oat fiber

eight to twelve ounces of water or hot or iced green tea with honey

Before Bed

Drink eight to twelve ounces of water or hot green tea with honey.

Exercise: go for a walk outdoors or participate in a favorite sport or recreational activity.

Supplements: make a drink with one tablespoon of organic raw apple cider vinegar and two teaspoons of raw organic honey dissolved in twelve ounces of warm purified water. Drink while taking two capsules of a systemic enzyme blend with proteases, bromelain, and papain. (For recommended products, visit www.BiblicalHealthInstitute.com and click on the Resource Guide.)

Advanced hygiene: follow the advanced hygiene recommendations from the morning of Day 1.

Emotional health: follow the forgiveness recommendations from the evening of Day 1.

Purpose: ask yourself these questions: "Did I live a life of purpose today?" "What did I do to add value to someone else's life today?" Commit to living a day of purpose tomorrow.

Prayer: thank God for this day, asking Him to give you a restoring night's rest and a fresh start tomorrow. Thank Him for His steadfast love that never ceases and His mercies that are new every morning. Read Psalm 23 aloud.

Body therapy: spend ten minutes listening to soothing music before you retire.

Sleep: go to bed by 10:30 p.m.

DAY 7

Upon Waking

Prayer: thank God because this is the day that the Lord has made. Rejoice and be glad in it. Thank Him for the breath in your lungs and the life in your body. Read Psalm 91 aloud.

Purpose: ask the Lord to give you an opportunity to add significance to someone's life today. Watch for that opportunity. Ask God to use you this day for His intended purpose.

Advanced hygiene: follow the advanced hygiene recommendations from Day 1.

Reduce toxins: follow the recommendations for reducing toxins from Day 1.

Supplements: make a drink with one tablespoon of organic raw apple cider vinegar and two teaspoons of raw organic honey dissolved in twelve ounces of warm purified water. Drink while taking two capsules of a systemic enzyme blend with proteases, bromelain, and papain. (For recommended products, visit www.BiblicalHealthInstitute.com and click on the Resource Guide.)

Exercise: perform functional fitness exercises for five to fifteen minutes or spend five to fifteen minutes on a mini trampoline. Finish with five to ten minutes of deep-breathing exercises.

Body therapy: get twenty minutes of direct sunlight sometime during the day, but be careful between the hours of 10:00 a.m. and 2:00 p.m.

Emotional health: follow the emotional health recommendations from the morning of Day 1.

Breakfast

Make a smoothie in a blender with the following ingredients:

1 cup plain yogurt or kefir (goat's milk is best)

1 tablespoon organic flaxseed oil

1 to 2 tablespoons organic raw honey

1 cup organic fruit (berries, banana, peaches, pineapple, etc.)

2 tablespoons goat's milk protein powder

dash of vanilla extract (optional)

Supplements: take two whole food multivitamin caplets and two capsules of a natural non-shellfish glucosamine product with *Boswellia serrata,* ginger, and turmeric.

Lunch

Before eating, drink eight ounces of water.

During lunch, drink eight ounces of water or hot or iced green tea with honey.

large green salad with mixed greens, avocado, carrots, tomato, red cabbage, red onions, red peppers, and sprouts with three ounces of cold, poached, or canned wild-caught salmon

salad dressing: mix extra virgin olive oil, apple cider vinegar or lemon juice, minced fresh garlic, naturally brewed soy sauce, Celtic Sea Salt, herbs, and spices; or, mix one tablespoon of extra virgin olive oil with one tablespoon of a healthy store-bought dressing

one piece of fruit in season

Supplements: take two whole food multivitamin caplets and two capsules of a natural non-shellfish glucosamine product with *Boswellia serrata,* ginger, and turmeric.

Dinner

Before eating, drink eight ounces of water.

During dinner, drink hot green tea with honey.

baked or grilled fish of your choice

steamed broccoli

baked sweet potato with butter

large green salad with mixed greens, avocado, carrots, tomato, red cabbage, red onions, red peppers, and sprouts

salad dressing: mix extra virgin olive oil, apple cider vinegar or lemon juice, minced fresh garlic, naturally brewed soy sauce, Celtic Sea Salt, herbs, and spices; or, mix one tablespoon of extra virgin olive oil with one tablespoon of a healthy store-bought dressing

Supplements: take two whole food multivitamin caplets and two capsules of a natural non-shellfish glucosamine product with *Boswellia serrata,* ginger, and turmeric with one to three teaspoons or three to nine capsules of a high omega-3 cod-liver oil complex.

Snacks

apple slices with raw sesame butter (tahini)

one berry antioxidant whole food nutrition bar with beta-glucans from soluble oat fiber

eight to twelve ounces of water or hot or iced green tea with honey

Before Bed

Drink eight to twelve ounces of water or hot or iced green tea with honey.

Exercise: go for a walk outdoors or participate in a favorite sport or recreational activity.

Supplements: make a drink with one tablespoon of organic raw apple cider vinegar and two teaspoons of raw organic honey dissolved in twelve ounces of warm purified water. Drink while taking two capsules of a systemic enzyme blend with proteases, bromelain, and papain. (For recommended products, visit www.BiblicalHealthInstitute.com and click on the Resource Guide.)

Advanced hygiene: follow the advanced hygiene recommendations from the morning of Day 1.

Emotional health: follow the forgiveness recommendations from the evening of Day 1.

Body therapy: take a warm bath for fifteen minutes with eight drops of biblical essential oils added.

Purpose: ask yourself these questions: "Did I live a life of purpose today?" "What did I do to add value to someone else's life today?" Commit to living a day of purpose tomorrow.

Prayer: thank God for this day, asking Him to give you a restoring night's rest and a fresh start tomorrow. Thank Him for His steadfast love that never ceases and His mercies that are new every morning. Read 1 Corinthians 13:4–8 aloud.

Sleep: go to bed by 10:30 p.m.

DAY 8 AND BEYOND

If you're feeling better, you can repeat the Great Physician's prescription for Arthritis Battle Plan as many times as you'd like. For detailed step-by-step suggestions and meal and lifestyle plans, visit www.BiblicalHealthInstitute.com and join the 40 Day Health Experience for continued good health. Or you may be interested in the Lifetime of Wellness plan if you want to maintain your newfound level of health. These online programs will provide you with customized daily meal and exercise plans and give you the tools to track your progress.

Need Recipes?

For a detailed list of over two hundred healthy and delicious recipes contained in the Great Physician's Rx eating plan, please visit www.BiblicalHealthInstitute.com.

NOTES

Introduction

1. "Arthritis: Keeping Your Joints Healthy," Harvard Medical School, http://www.health.harvard.edu/special_health_reports/Arthritis.htm (accessed April 5, 2007).
2. "Arthritis: A Chronic and Disabling Condition" (Washington, D. C.: National Academy on an Aging Society, 2000), based on interviews conducted by the National Center for Health Statistics.
3. "A Closer Look at Arthritis," Arthritis Foundation and National Pharmaceutical Council, http://www.npcnow.org/resources/PDFs/CL_Arthritis.pdf (accessed April 9, 2007).
4. Ibid.
5. "Osteoarthritis Health Center," WebMD, http://www.webmd.com/diseases_and_conditions/osteoarthritis.htm (accessed April 5, 2007).
6. National Institute of Arthritis and Musculoskeletal and Skin Diseases, *Handout on Health: Osteoarthritis*, NIH Publication No. 02-4617, July 2002.
7. Michael T. Murray, ND, and Joseph E. Pizzorno, ND, *Encyclopedia of Natural Medicine* (New York: Three Rivers Press, 1998), 696.
8. "Knee & Hip Replacement: The Safer Cutting Edge," Onlypunjab.com, http://www.onlypunjab.com/fitness/fullstory-insight-fitness+healthcare-newsID-10134.html (accessed April 5, 2007).
9. Bill Pennington, "Baby Boomers Stay Active, and So Do Their Doctors," *New York Times*, April 16, 2006.
10. Paul Schulick, *Ginger: Common Spice & Wonder Drug*, 3rd. ed. (Prescott, Ariz.: Hohm Press, 1996), 32.
11. Pfizer Inc., "Investor News Release," http://www.pfizer.com/pfizer/are/investors_releases/2006pr/mn_2006_0419.jsp, April 16, 2006.

12. "Live From," CNN, http://transcripts.cnn.com/TRANSCRIPTS/0412/17/lol.02.html (accessed April 5, 2007).
13. "Arthritis Diet Remedies: Fact or Folklore," *PDR Family Guide to Nutrition and Health* (Thomson Healthcare, 2004).
14. Hershel Sarbin and Jim Brown, "Golf After 50," PGATour.com, http://www.pgatour.com/story/6142931 (accessed January 22, 2003).

Key #1

1. David Williamson, "Study Reveals Possible Link Between Osteoarthritis, Diet," UNC-CH News, http://www.unc.edu/news/archives/nov98/jordan.htm (accessed April 5, 2007).
2. Eugene Zampieron, ND, and Ellen Kamhi, Ph.D., *Arthritis: An Alternative Medicine Definitive Guide* (Tiburon, Calif.: AlternativeMedicine.com Books, 1999), 250.
3. Zampieron and Kamhi, *Arthritis,* 251.
4. Sally Fallon with Mary G. Enig, Ph.D., *Nourishing Traditions: The Cookbook that Challenges Politically Correct Nutrition and the Diet Dictocrats* (Winona Lake, Ind.: NewTrends Publishing, 2000).
5. Zampieron and Kamhi, *Arthritis,* 251.
6. Jason Theodosakis, M.D., Brenda Adderly, MHA, and Barry Fox, Ph.D., *The Arthritis Cure* (New York: St. Martin's Press, 1997), 169.
7. Nichola Groom, "Atkins Files for Bankruptcy as Low-Carb Slumps," Reuters News Service, August 1, 2005.
8. "Chicken Soup, Rx for the Cold," Health A to Z, http://www.healthatoz.com/healthatoz/Atoz/dc/caz/resp/cold/chixsoup.jsp (accessed April 5, 2007).
9. Jean-Jacques Dugoua, ND, "Chicken Soup for Your Joints," Truestar Health, http://www.truestarhealth.com/members/cm_archives07ML4P1A2.html (accessed April 5, 2007).
10. Reuters News Service, "Eating Fruits and Vegetables May Cut Arthritis Risk: Study," August 17, 2005.
11. Harris H. McIlwain, M.D., and Debra Fulghum Bruce, MS, "The Pain-Free Arthritis Diet," Buzzle.com, http://www.buzzle.com/editorials/10-4-2003-46153.asp (accessed April 5, 2007).

12. Schulick, *Ginger: Common Spice & Wonder Drug*, 37.
13. F. Batmanghelidj, M.D., *You're Not Sick, You're Thirsty!* (New York: Warner Books, 2003), 150.
14. "Green Tea May Prevent Arthritis Says Sheffield Scientist," Arthritis Research Campaign (ARC), http://www.arc.org.uk/news/pressreleases/results/greentea.asp (accessed April 9, 2007).
15. Phyllis A. Balch, CNC, *Prescription for Nutritional Healing* (New York: Avery, 2000), 190.

Key #2

1. "Looking for a Natural Remedy?" Arthritis Foundation, http://www.arthritis.org/conditions/supplementguide (accessed April 5, 2007).
2. Richard Harkness, "Results of Glucosamine, Chondroitin NIH Trials Are Hazy," Knight Ridder News Service, May 9, 2006.
3. "High-Dose Vitamin D Supplements Act as Anti-Inflammatory," NutraIngredients.com, http://www.nutraingredients-usa.com/news/ng.asp?n=66953-vitamin-d-inflammation-chf (accessed April 10, 2007).
4. V. P. Billigmann, "Enzyme Therapy: An Alternative in Treatment of Herpes Zoster. A Controlled Study of 192 Patients [translated from German]," *Fortschritte der Medizin* 113 (1995): 43–48.
5. Judith Horstman, "Ayurvedic Herbs," *Arthritis Today*, http://www.arthritis.org/resources/arthritistoday/1999_archives/1999_05_06explorations.asp (accessed April 5, 2007).
6. Reuters News Service, "Study of Cyanotech's BioAstin Natural Astaxanthin Indicates Significant Reduction," http://today.reuters.com/stocks/QuoteCompanyNewsArticle.aspx?view=PR&symbol=CYAN.O&storyID=175133+02-Mar-2006+BW (accessed March 2, 2006).
7. "More Support for Vitamin K's Protection from Osteoarthritis," NutraIngredients.com, http://www.nutraingredients-usa.com/news/ng.asp?id=67028-vitamin-k-osteoarthritis-rhematism (accessed April 9, 2007).

Key #3

1. Kenneth E. Seaton, Ph.D., DSc, *Life, Health, and Longevity* (Scientific Hygiene, 1994), 47.

Key #4

1. "Super-Secret Phone Calls Revealed! (Thank you, domestic spying.)," Fox Sports, feed://community.foxsports.com/blogs/cloudmark?RSS (accessed April 9, 2007).
2. "Arthritis: Exercise to Treat Arthritis," WebMD, http://www.webmd.com/content/article/78/95590.htm (accessed April 5, 2007).
3. "Hydrotherapy Helpful in Osteoarthritis," Medscape Today from WebMD, http://www.medscape.com/viewarticle/465053 (accessed April 11, 2007).

Key #5

1. Press Release, "New Study to Improve Understanding of Osteoarthritis," Duke University, http://www.pratt.duke.edu/news/?id=127 (accessed April 5, 2007).
2. Press Release, "New Study to Improve the Understanding of Osteoarthritis," Duke University, http://www.dukemednews.org/news/article.php?id=7246 (accessed April 5, 2007).

Key #6

1. Norman Cousins, "The Laughter Connection," http://www.sociology.ccsu.edu/ertel/cousins.htm (accessed April 5, 2007).

About the Authors

Jordan Rubin has dedicated his life to transforming the health of God's people one life at a time. He is the founder and chairman of Garden of Life, Inc., a health and wellness company based in West Palm Beach, Florida, that produces organic functional foods, whole food nutritional supplements and personal care products, and he is a much-in-demand speaker on various health topics.

He and his wife, Nicki, are the parents of a toddler-aged son, Joshua. They make their home in Palm Beach Gardens, Florida.

Joseph D. Brasco, M.D., who has extensive knowledge and experience in gastroenterology and internal medicine, attended medical school at Medical College of Wisconsin in Milwaukee, Wisconsin, and is board certified with the American Board of Internal Medicine. Besides writing for various medical journals, he is also the coauthor of *Restoring Your Digestive Health* with Jordan Rubin. Dr. Brasco is currently in private practice in Huntsville, Alabama.